Lament for a Nation

CARLETON LIBRARY SERIES

The Carleton Library Series, funded by Carleton University under the general editorship of the dean of the School of Graduate Studies and Research, publishes books about Canadian economics, geography, history, politics, society, and related subjects. It includes important new works as well as reprints of classics in the fields. The editorial committee welcomes manuscripts and suggestions, which should be sent to the dean of the School of Graduate Studies and Research, Carleton University.

GEORGE GRANT

Lament for a Nation

THE DEFEAT OF CANADIAN NATIONALISM

Carleton Library Series 205

McGILL-QUEEN'S UNIVERSITY PRESS
MONTREAL & KINGSTON • LONDON • ITHACA

ISBN 978-0-7735-3002-7 (cloth)
ISBN 978-0-7735-3010-2 (paper)

Printed and bound in Canada
Reprinted 2007

McGill-Queen's University Press acknowledges the financial support of the
Government of Canada through the Book Publishing Industry Development
Program (BPIDP) for its activities. It also acknowledges the support of the
Canada Council for the Arts for its publishing program.

LIBRARY AND ARCHIVES CANADA CATALOGUING IN PUBLICATION

Grant George, 1918-1988
    Lament for a nation: the defeat of Canadian nationalism / George
Grant. – 40th anniversary ed.

(The Carleton library series ; 205)
Includes bibliographical references.
ISBN 978-0-7735-3002-7 (bnd)
ISBN 978-0-7735-3010-2 (pbk)

    1. Nationalism – Canada.   2. Canada – Politics and government.
3. Canada – Relations – United States.   4. United States – Relations –
Canada.   5. Conservatism – Canada.   6. Liberalism – Canada.   I. Title.
II. Series: Carleton library ; 205
FC97.G7 2005   971.064   C2005-906266-5

Contents

To Derek Bedson and Judith Robinson

TWO LOVERS OF THEIR COUNTRY

ONE LIVING AND ONE DEAD

Introduction to the 40th Anniversary Edition

ANDREW POTTER

The impossibility of conservatism in our era is the impossibility of Canada. As Canadians we attempted a ridiculous task in trying to build a conservative nation in the age of progress, on a continent we share with the most dynamic nation on earth. The current of modern history is against us.

George Grant, *Lament for a Nation*

A political philosopher who spent his most productive years teaching in a department of religion, George Grant is probably best known today as the father of English-speaking Canadian nationalism. He earned this reputation, somewhat curiously, thanks to *Lament for a Nation*, which declared that Canada had ceased to exist as a sovereign country. First published in 1965, *Lament for a Nation* remains George Grant's most enduring and most important work. It is the sun under which a generation of Canadian nationalists warm themselves, but it also casts the long dark shadows in which they must operate.

For anyone interested in the ongoing questions of Canadian identity, sovereignty, and national unity, the book remains essential reading. In his Forward to the 1997 edition of *Lament for a Nation*, Peter C. Emberly says that the book "should be respected as a masterpiece of political meditation."[1] As he goes on to point out, the job of a meditation is to take the reader from the familiar and the near to more enduring and abstract forms of understanding. Yet much has changed in Canada and in North America over the past forty years, with over half the population born since 1965. What was familiar and near to the Canada of the mid 1960s is now in the distant and receding past. This introduction provides some historical, political, and intellectual context to allow contemporary readers to better understand and critically assess the book's central arguments.

THE RISE AND FALL OF JOHN DIEFENBAKER

Canadians have relatively few binding national myths, but one of the most pervasive and enduring is the conviction that the country is doomed. Confederation has always seemed like a rather rickety, precarious endeavour, perpetually on the verge of fragmenting into a handful of region-states or surrendering to outright absorption or annexation by the United States. An immense, underpopulated country, sharing a border, history, language, and culture with the great republican experiment to the south, Canada is not an easy country to govern or in which to promote a distinct national identity. Canadians have always felt the centrifugal tug of conflicting loyalties – to Britain, to Quebec or a particular region, or even to the United States – and these have often seemed strong enough to pull the country apart. As the novelist Robertson Davies famously put it, Canada "is not a country you love, it is a country you worry about."

As a political entity, Canada began as a collection of British colonies and even after Confederation remained culturally, economically, and politically dependent on Great Britain. It was only after World War I that Canada began to come into its own as a nation, taking a steps that led to steadily greater independence from Britain. At the Paris Peace Conference of 1919, Prime Minister Robert Borden won separate representation for the Canadian delegation, although Britain ultimately signed the final treaty on behalf of the whole Empire. Under the subsequent leadership of Prime Minister Mackenzie King, Canada continued to push for a reappraisal of the constitutional relationship between Britain and the dominions. The Imperial Conference of 1926, chaired by Lord Balfour, resulted in a declaration that the various dominions were "autonomous Communities within the British Empire, equal in status, in no way subordinate to one another in any aspect of their domestic or external affairs, though united by a common allegiance to the Crown, and freely associated as members of the British Commonwealth of Nations." This had the effect of freeing the dominions from British foreign policy and was followed by the 1931 Statute of Westminster, which granted them full legislative freedom from Westminster.[2]

If World War I freed Canada from the British embrace, the imperatives of World War II demanded close economic and military ties between Canada and the United States. After the stunning Nazi victories early in the war, Britain found itself alone in Europe, and the Liberal Prime Minister Mackenzie King soon realized that Canada – with just over 11 million citizens – was Britain's largest remaining ally. In August 1940, King met with President Roosevelt at Ogdensberg, New York, where they agreed to set up a Permanent Joint Board on Defence. This committed Canada to intimate and ongoing military ties with the United States. The continental economy became highly integrated in the name of wartime production and for many Canadians it appeared that the country had escaped one empire only to plunge into the orbit of another. As Harold Innis remarked to a British audience in 1949, in a few short years Canada had moved "from colony to nation to colony."

Innis's statement has become a cliché, but it survives because

Canadians have found it a useful way of describing their situation, perched historically and geographically between two great English-speaking empires. After World War II, the Cold War put a damper on any pretensions of independence in military or foreign relations. Quebecers remained caught in the combined grip of the clergy and Maurice Duplessis, and English Canadians were absorbed with the task of rebuilding the economy and re-integrating the returning veterans.

The country awoke in mid-century to the realization that it was being economically and culturally absorbed by the United States. Starting with the Royal Commission on National Development in the Arts, Letters and Sciences (commonly known as the Massey Commission), Canadians began to examine ways of meeting the challenge of defining and defending a distinct national culture that would in turn serve as the basis of a unique Canadian identity. The economic program was a harder sell, but in 1956 the Gordon Royal Commission on Canada's Economic Prospects recommended a mild program of economic nationalism, which was ignored by the Liberal Prime Minister Louis St. Laurent and his pro-business "minister of everything," C.D. Howe.

For Canadians, the 1950s were a period of somewhat desultory national soul-searching, and the country approached its centennial in a mood of growing collective self-doubt. The Liberals had been in power since 1935 and seemed destined to remain so under the avuncular leadership of Louis St. Laurent. The Progressive Conservatives were led by John Diefenbaker, a former defence lawyer from Prince Albert, Saskatchewan, who was noted for his excellent public-speaking skills and his inability to win elections. Diefenbaker had lost repeatedly at every level of government until he finally won a seat in Parliament in 1940. He then failed in two bids to become leader of the Progressive Conservative party before winning the job in 1956.

The 1957 general election was supposed to be a sleepwalk to victory for the Liberals, but Diefenbaker had other ideas. With spectacular, urgent oratory, he fashioned a personality cult of sorts around the campaign slogan "It's Time for a Diefenbaker Government." Railing against the arrogant, contemptuous Liberals, "The Chief" made a non-partisan appeal directly to the people, asking Canadians to join him in the fulfillment of Canada's destiny. He saw himself as a true nation-builder, the only legitimate heir to Sir John A. Macdonald: "I am one of those who believe this party has a sacred trust, a trust in accordance with the traditions of Macdonald. It has an appointment today with destiny, to plan and build for a greater Canada ... one Canada, with equality of opportunity for every citizen and equality for every province from the Atlantic to the Pacific."[3]

The Progressive Conservatives surprised everyone by winning a minority government. After an energetic and popular year in power, Diefenbaker went to the people once again. In the 1958 election he supplanted his "One Canada" appeal with what he called "The Vision," a magnificently vague platform of land conservation, economic policy, road construction, and the "completion" of Confederation through the development of a self-governing North. But, once again, it was the manner of the appeal that was the real content and the country returned Diefenbaker's government to power, sending 208 Conservatives to Ottawa, at that time the largest majority in Canadian history.

Diefenbaker was unable to transfer the rhetoric into reality. Apparently unwilling to use his massive majority to push ahead with the reforms the country needed, Diefenbaker soon established a reputation as disorganized and a ditherer. He was distrustful of the Ottawa bureaucracy and unable to give his cabinet the discipline and direction it needed. He divided his caucus, alienated his supporters, and caused the country's financial establishment to turn its back on the party.

There were a few successes. Diefenbaker was a big fan of the Commonwealth, and at a Prime Ministers' Conference in London in 1961 he was instrumental in forcing South Africa – with its racist apartheid regime – out of the organization. He also gave Canada a Bill of Rights, extended the federal franchise to natives, and appointed Georges Vanier as the country's first French-Canadian governor general. Yet these achievements, minor even on their own terms, were overshadowed by a steady succession of crises, the worst of them concerning foreign policy.

In 1957 Diefenbaker made a hasty decision to join the North American Air Defence Command (NORAD), a Canada-US air defence alliance that integrated the air defence forces of Canada and the US under a joint command based in Colorado. With hardly any public debate or discussion in Cabinet, Diefenbaker committed Canada to accepting nuclear weapons, a position that subsequently divided the government and the country. On the 20th of February 1959 he cancelled the Avro Arrow supersonic fighter project on the grounds that the plane was both too expensive and obsolete. This may have been a sound decision, but it was poorly handled and alienated many Canadians, as well as sending thousands of Canadian scientists and engineers to the United States.

The previous fall the Diefenbaker government had asked the Americans for two squadrons of Bomarc antiaircraft missiles, one to be based at North Bay, Ontario, the other at La Macaza, Quebec, after it realized that the American antiaircraft line, being deployed along the border, could result in nuclear warfare being fought in the skies over the Windsor-Quebec City corridor. The government had not, however, made it clear to Canadians that these missiles would them-

selves be equipped with nuclear warheads. When this information came to light in 1960, it sparked a furious public
debate over whether Canada should become a nuclear power.
Ultimately, the government found itself unable to accept
either the nuclear warheads the missiles required or the
American soldiers who would need to be stationed in Canada
to guard the warheads. The upshot of all of this was that
Canada had spent hundreds of millions of dollars on useless
weapons systems.

It hadn't done much for Canada-US relations either, and
things only got worse during the 1962 Cuban Missile Crisis.
After aerial photographs and other intelligence suggested that
the USSR was moving ballistic missiles into Cuba, President
John F. Kennedy ordered a naval blockade of the island. He
also ordered NORAD to a "Defcon 3" alert status, giving
Diefenbaker only an hour and a half notice. Bitter at not
having been properly consulted, Diefenbaker and his secretary of state for external affairs, Howard Green, were reluc-
tant to comply with the request. Worried about offending the
USSR, they raised doubts about the actual existence of the
missiles. The crisis played itself out while a divided cabinet
debated what to do; by the time Diefenbaker ordered the
alert on 24 October 1962, the Soviet ships steaming toward
the American blockade had turned around, avoiding a potential military confrontation.

These events contributed to a growing sense that Diefenbaker's government was both indecisive and anti-American.
It also led to what many historians see as unprecedented
interference by the Americans in Canadian politics. Diefenbaker had survived the 1962 June election with a minority
government. In January 1963 U.S. General Lauris Norstad
gave a press conference in Ottawa where he openly rebuked
the Diefenbaker government for its indecisiveness. In retalia-
tion, Canada recalled Charles Ritchie, its ambassador in

Washington. With half the cabinet in revolt and the media in a frenzy, Liberal leader Lester B. Pearson called for a non-confidence vote in Parliament. The government soon fell.

In the ensuing election Diefenbaker fought an amazing campaign. "Everybody's against me but the people," he said, and he traveled the country relentlessly, everywhere portraying himself as a tragic figure battling alone against the Canadian establishment and its shadowy American overlords. He almost won the election single-handedly, but he had lost the support of the financial community on Bay Street in Toronto. Quebecers had never been fond of his "one nation" vision, which was unsympathetic to the province's distinct nature, and the Progressive Conservatives were almost completely wiped out in that province. Meanwhile, Pearson jumped on the defence policy crisis, arguing that, thanks to a rudderless and out-of-control government, Canada was forfeiting its position as a player on the world stage. Pearson won a minority government and once in power decided to accept warheads for nuclear-capable forces. The Bomarc warheads arrived at their sites on 31 December 1963.

THE INEVITABLE DISAPPEARANCE OF CANADA

The fall of the Progressive Conservative government in 1963 and the restoration of the Liberal party under Pearson provide the immediate political backdrop to George Grant's *Lament for a Nation*. Pearson's willingness to accept nuclear warheads and generally accommodate the Americans gives the book its intellectual motivation. And Diefenbaker's perceived shabby treatment at the hands of the "Canadian elite" gives it its overtones of seething, focused anger. The book opens with a broadside of indignation:

Never has such a torrent of abuse been poured on any Canadian figure as that during the years from 1960 to 1965. Never have the wealthy and the clever been so united as they were in their joint attack on Mr. John Diefenbaker. It has made life pleasant for the literate classes to know that they were on the winning side. Emancipated journalists were encouraged to express their dislike of the small-town Protestant politician, and they knew they would be well paid by the powerful for their efforts. Suburban matrons and professors knew that there was an open season on Diefenbaker, and that jokes against him at cocktail parties would guarantee the medal of sophistication. (3)[4]

What was it about Diefenbaker's attempt at governing Canada that "turned the ruling class into a pack howling for his blood"? (4). According to Grant, the tragedy of John G. Diefenbaker is merely a symptom of our true condition, which involves the inevitable disappearance of Canada as a sovereign country. It is because Canada is destined to die that the book is a lament: "To lament is to cry out at the death or dying of something loved. This lament mourns the end of Canada as a sovereign state" (4).

It might seem strange, even a bit hysterical, to suggest that the transfer of power from one political party to another leaves Canadian nationalists gasping for air "like fish left on the shores of a drying lake" (5). For Grant, this is the case because Canadians made the mistake of seeing Diefenbaker's failures as a function of his personality. For example, in *Renegade in Power* Peter C. Newman focuses almost entirely on Diefenbaker's egomania, paranoia, and indecisiveness. On this view, what went wrong, ultimately, was that Diefenbaker did not have the courage to follow through in public on his private convictions. As Newman writes, "he gave us a leadership cult, without the leadership."[5]

George Grant argued that the problem went deeper. He believed that Diefenbaker's downfall was not due to defects in his personality but in his principles. He lost because his attempt at promoting a conservative form of nationalism was at odds with the fundamentally liberal character of the country's ruling elites. As a small-town lawyer from the prairies, Diefenbaker never quite grasped how much Canada had changed since the inter-war period, how the members of the establishment no longer had an instinctive loyalty to Great Britain. Thanks to the integrationist policies put in motion by Mackenzie King and entrenched by C.D. Howe, the country was now an economic and political appendage of the United States, so much so that "the Canadian ruling class looks across the border for its final authority in both politics and culture" (9). According to Grant, Diefenbaker's mistake was in seeing his colossal majority as the result of more than just a desire to teach the Liberals a lesson. He mistook it for a hunger for a new nationalism and a revitalized sense of national purpose and destiny.

Grant sees Diefenbaker's conservative form of nationalism as made up of three elements: a grassroots prairie populism, a faith in private enterprise, and a connection to old-fashioned Toryism and Britain. This is a strange mixture and Grant argues that the attempt to hold these together only led to confusion. The free-enterprise ideology was at odds with the older Conservative party, the one that "created Ontario Hydro, the CNR, the Bank of Canada, and the CBC" (15). The populist impulse was completely inadequate to the post-war demands of a bureaucratized, industrialized mass society. Populism belonged "to the Saskatchewan or Wisconsin of Diefenbaker's youth, not to those who work for Simpson's-Sears or General Motors" (14). Meanwhile, the British connection was already dying by the time Diefenbaker came to power, a vestigial organ in an increasingly North Americanized body politic.

The problems went beyond the contradictory elements of Diefenbaker's native nationalism. He also failed to take the steps necessary to consolidate his power and defend the national interest. Most importantly for Grant, Diefenbaker didn't seem to appreciate the extent to which Canada's survival depended on some form of socialism. To reverse the steady integration of the Great Lakes region into the United States, Diefenbaker "would have had to appeal over the heads of corporation capitalism to the masses of Ontario and Quebec" (16). Instead, he managed the double fumble of both refusing to advance any serious program of economic nationalism while still managing to antagonize the centres of financial power in Montreal and Toronto.

More bewildering, according to Grant, was Diefenbaker's failure to find an effective Quebec lieutenant. Ever since the great alliance of Sir John A. Macdonald and George Etienne Cartier, the Conservatives had recognized the importance of cooperating "with those who seek the continuance of the Franco-American [Quebecois] civilization" (21) It did not help that the Progressive Conservative party's natural allies in Quebec, the Union Nationale, were rocked by the death of their leader, Maurice Duplessis, in 1959, and, four months later, by that of his successor, Paul Sauvé.

Grant also chides Diefenbaker for his anti-intellectualism and for turning his back on his natural allies in the universities. By the 1960s there was a generation of committed conservative nationalist intellectuals writing extensively on modernity and its effect on Canada. This group included heavyweights like W.L. Morton, Northrop Frye, and Donald Creighton, but instead of drawing on them to help give his government some intellectual cement, Diefenbaker relied on party hacks and political cronies. The upshot was that in the 1963 election "Diefenbaker had no support from the intellectual community, although he was standing on the attractive platform of Canadian sovereignty. This is a measure of how far he had carried yahooism in his years of office" (25).

The first three chapters of *Lament* are a resounding indictment of Diefenbaker's government. What redeems Diefenbaker in Grant's eyes, as both a nationalist and a leader, is the prime minister's courage in finally standing up to the Americans over defence issues. As Grant sees it, in refusing to blindly submit to American demands during the Cuban Missile Crisis, Diefenbaker had taken the strongest stand ever attempted by a Canadian government against American-satellite status, such that "Nothing in Diefenbaker's ministry was as noble as his leaving of it" (26).

Grant interprets the events of 1962–63 as a sustained attempt by the United States, supported by the Canadian defence establishment, the newspapers, and the civil service in Ottawa, at bringing down an excessively nationalist and insufficiently cooperative government. The mistake Diefenbaker made was in assuming that Canada was a sovereign country and that its defence policy would be made in Ottawa. Furthermore, he did not appreciate how continentalist the entire country had become, how its branch-plant economy had created a branch-plant culture: "Most Canadians were as convinced as the American public that Kennedy had been right doing what he did in Cuba, and that his actions showed the wisdom of 'decisiveness' in foreign policy. So 'decisiveness' was subtly identified with Canada's need to have arms" (32).[6]

Ultimately, Grant sees the sincerity of Diefenbaker's nationalism in the fact that he stood up to the Americans, stood up to the Canadian establishment, and stood by his external affairs minister Howard Green (who railed against Canada becoming a "vassal") even when it was in his manifest interest to do otherwise. Even so, "it took the full weight of the North-American establishment to bring him down" (28).

Thus Diefenbaker's stand was the last gasp of Canadian nationalism. Given that the country seems condemned to be ruled by the continentalist Liberals, Grant wonders whether there is anything that could justify the Liberal party from a nationalist perspective. He considers three possibilities.

First, we could appreciate the Liberals as the party of realistic nationalism, working to keep the country as Canadian as possible under the circumstances. A second argument might be that it is inevitable that Canada will become part of the United States; the virtue of the Liberals is that they see this and are willing to make the transition as smooth as possible. Finally, it could be that Canada's disappearance is not just necessary but *good*, and so we should be grateful to the Liberals for leading us to wider, richer horizons.[7]

The first argument is the one that the Liberals usually advance in their own defence. On economic and military matters, the party claims that it has always understood the realities of sharing a tent with the Americans, that Canada simply cannot pretend that the country sits anywhere other than stretched across the top half of the North American continent. Domestically, the Liberals' republican hostility to the British connection – demonstrated through policies such as the adoption of the Maple Leaf (1965) and the changing of Dominion Day to Canada Day (1982) – stems from a deep understanding of Quebec's status as "the keystone of Confederation." Keeping Quebec happy is paramount, even if it means that English Canada must turn its back on its own symbols, traditions, and values.

Grant doesn't buy this. When he looks at what the Liberal party has actually done on the nationalist front, he sees that every policy they have ever endorsed has ensured the country's eventual demise: "It was under a Liberal régime that Canada became a branch-plant society; it was under Liberal leadership that our independence in defence and foreign

affairs was finally broken ... it is absurd to argue that the
Liberals have been successful nationalists" (40). The decisive
period was from 1940–57, when King permanently yoked
the defence of Canada to the defence of the United States and
C.D. Howe ensured the full integration of the continental
economy. The best Grant will say for the Liberals, then, is
that they have made the patient's death relatively painless.

The question is, was Canada's death necessary? Did the
country ever have an alternative future? Grant discusses a couple of options. One would have been to follow Castro's lead in
Cuba: Canada could have established a communist state and
turned to the Soviets for support. A second possibility would
have been to attempt something like what De Gaulle accomplished in France, using the nationalism of the country's elites
to put strict limits on foreign capital, technology, and influence. This was more or less the idea behind Macdonald's
National Policy of 1878, which used a high tariff wall to protect domestic manufacturers. It was the basis of Conservative
policy for decades and was buttressed by other interventionist
initiatives, including national development projects such as the
building of the CPR and the settlement of the West.

Castroism was never a serious option, for obvious reasons.
Canadians were simply not sufficiently socialist, and, even if
they had been, the Americans would never have permitted a
pro-Soviet government to exist along their entire northern
border. Gaullism ceased to function after World War II, when
it was no longer "in the interests of the economically powerful to be nationalists." With the diminished tug of trade with
Britain and the absence of anything like the National Policy,
Canadian capitalists found that their interests directed their
attention southward, and since for Grant they were nothing
but money-grubbers, "They lost nothing essential to the principle of their lives in losing their country" (46).

Grant is hard on his country's capitalist class, but he is even harder on its civil service. He argues that by the 1960s a profoundly continentalist orientation had spread to the political mandarins in Ottawa. While he concedes that it would be wrong to question the loyalty of senior civil servants such as Mitchell Sharp, Robert Bryce, and Norman Robertson, he remarks backhandedly that "they were not the diamond stuff of which nationalists must be made in these circumstances" (48). Their failure was one of attention, since they did not appear to recognize what was required to preserve Canada's independence. The problem, argues Grant, was that Canada's senior officials had stopped thinking like Canadians and had become "more and more representative of a western empire than civil servants of a particular nation state ... They identified themselves with the international community rather than nationalist 'hayseeds' such as Green and Diefenbaker. In the final analysis, they were provincial servants of the greatest empire since Rome" (51).

If this critique of the Canadian civil service seems a bit unfair (and more than a bit condescending), in the end Grant appears willing to let them off the hook. In chapter 5 of *Lament* he suggests that Canada has been defeated not by problems of language and geography, nor by capitalist self-interest and bureaucratic ineptitude. Instead, it has been done in by nothing less than the very character of modernity. The essence of modernity is "progress," which is understood as the conquest, exploitation, and control of nature through science. The argument for why Canada must disappear in an age of progress proceeds as follows:

1 The modern (technological) world evolves inexorably towards the "universal and homogeneous state," which renders local cultures redundant.

2 Canada is a local culture situated next to the very heart of modernity, the technological dynamo of the United States.
3 Canadians think of modernity as a good thing.
Therefore,
4 Canada, even as understood by its own citizens, is redundant.

It is worth noting that the idea behind the first premise – that technology is a universal homogenizing force – was an almost uncriticized assumption in mainstream social sciences from the 1950s to the 1970s. It was accepted by most European thinkers, in particular the members of the 'Frankfurt school" (which included Theodor Adorno, Max Horkheimer, and Herbert Marcuse) as well as by American critics of "mass society" such as Daniel Bell, C. Wright Mills, and Theodore Roszak.

Grant's acceptance of this premise was in no way eccentric, and his originality lay in applying it directly to the Canadian political situation. On this view, it is not just Canada that is destined to disappear but all particular cultures, all "nations." Canada just happens to be the leading edge of that process thanks to its unique geographical and historical situation next to the United States.[8]

Grant writes that "the enterprise of western civilization finds its spearhead in the American empire."[9] America is the centre of a civilization that privileges a liberal ideology according to which "man's essence is his freedom. Nothing must stand in the way of our absolute freedom to create the world as we want it. There must be no conceptions of the good that put limitations on human action. The definition of man as freedom constitutes the heart of the age of progress. The doctrine of progress is not, as Marx believed, the perfectibility of man, but an open-ended progression in which men will be endlessly free to make the world as they want it" (55).

For Grant, one corollary of the liberal discourse of "freedom" is that it closes us off from any public conception of the good. Questions of "the good" are reduced to mere expressions of "values," which are necessarily private. Each of us is free to pursue our own conception of the good according to our chosen values, as long as this pursuit is consistent with an equal amount of freedom for everyone else. Rather tartly, Grant offers that, on this view, "Nobody minds if we prefer women or dogs or boys, as long as we cause no public inconvenience" (56). From this it follows that, in the age of progress, a conservative society, organized around values of hierarchy, deference, tradition, and public morality, is impossible. Which is bad news for Canada, because what made Confederation a morally valuable enterprise was that it expressed the joint desire of English- and French-speaking peoples in the Atlantic colonies and the Canadas to maintain their conservative traditions.

It is important to understand what Grant means when he suggests that Canada was an attempt at building a society *more* conservative than that of the United States. He notes that, on a certain reading, America can be seen as a conservative country. For all its violence, the American revolution was not about any great dispute over principle, since the revolutionaries saw themselves as demanding nothing more than the traditional rights of Englishmen, particularly the Lockean ideals of individual rights, property, and constitutional government. But if Lockeanism is what we mean by English-speaking conservatism, then what do we make of the Loyalists? After all, the standard understanding of their actions is that they fled to Canada precisely because they desired to live in a society more British, and more conservative, than the one which they fled.

Not wishing to deny the moral significance of Loyalism, Grant argues that they were appealing to an older, pre-

Lockean, form of conservatism rooted in the political philosophy of Richard Hooker (1554–1600). Hooker was an Elizabethan theologian, a Christian humanist who was a follower of Thomas Aquinas. At the heart of his political theory was the conviction that there had to be an intimate connection between the state and the church. Society would be ruled jointly by the secular government informed by natural law and by church as informed by revealed law. Grant says that that this brand of British conservatism is hard to articulate, "because it is less a clear view of existence than an appeal to an ill-defined past" (68). Nevertheless, among its principles we can discern a preference for a society built around a sense of community, public order, self-restraint, and loyalty to the state. In Canada, this finds expression in the opening words of section 91 of the Constitution Act, 1867, which gives Parliament the power to legislate for the "peace, order, and good government" of Canada, as well as in a general willingness to exercise centralized state control over political and economic development. As Grant is fond of pointing out, it was Conservative governments that created Ontario Hydro, the CBC, and the Canadian National Railway.

As for the French-Canadians, Grant argues that their loyalty to the British Crown from 1791[10] on was always strategic, useful only to the extent that it enabled them to preserve a Catholic society organized around an understanding of public virtue, in which individual freedoms are restricted in the name of the collective good. Under Premier Maurice Duplessis the influence of American corporations in Quebec was balanced by the extraordinary influence of the church, but with the end of the Duplessis regime and the rise of the provincial Liberals under Jean Lesage in 1960, responsibility for the preservation of the French fact began to shift from the church to the state. It was thanks to pressure from his minister of natural resources, René Lévesque, that Lesage nationalized the electricity companies, operating under the slogan "Maitre chez nous."

According to George Grant, the consequence of this semi-socialist statism can only be that for Quebec, "the continuance of Confederation is simply a question of convenience. If French civilization can be protected as a province within Confederation, then all well and good. If it cannot be, then separatism becomes a necessity" (75–6). On this view, Canada can only survive if both solitudes remain committed to the joint project of preserving their respective conservative traditions. Liberalism is an inherently universalizing and homogenizing creed, incompatible with the particular loyalty of nationalism, and even a separate language will not be able to save Quebec: "It is surely more than a language that Lévesque wishes to preserve in his nation. New Orleans is a pleasant place for tourists" (78).

And there ends the argument of *Lament for a Nation*. Canada makes sense only as a conservative country and Diefenbaker's stand was the last political gasp of conservatism in the face of the ineluctable fact that conservatism is not possible in North America in an age of progress. Canada's disappearance was inevitable. You can't fight necessity, because "Fate leads the willing, and drives the unwilling. The debt we owe the Liberals is that they have been so willing to be led. The party has been made up of those who put only one condition on their willingness: that they should have personal charge of the government while our sovereignty disappears" (85).

WHO WAS GEORGE GRANT?

As the book's title makes clear, the tone is one of lamentation, not provocation. George Grant did not intend *Lament*

for a Nation as a wake-up call to Canadian nationalists,
although that is the effect it had. In a frequently quoted
remark, the leftist nationalist James Laxer said that it was
"the most important book I ever read in my life. Here was a
crazy old philosopher of religion at McMaster and he woke
up half our generation."[11]

Yet in many ways it is not surprising that this "crazy old
philosopher" became the father of mid-century Canadian
nationalism, since George Parkin Grant was a member of the
closest thing that Canada has had to an indigenous English-
speaking aristocracy. His grandfather George Munro Grant
was principal of Queen's University from 1877 until his
death in 1902 and was responsible for turning a poor
denominational college into one of the country's finest and
best-endowed universities. His maternal grandfather was
George Parkin, leader of the Imperial Federation Movement
in the 1880s and principal of Upper Canada College (UCC)
from 1895 to 1902. Parkin later served in London as secretary of the Rhodes Scholarship Trust and was knighted for
his service to the Empire. Grant's father, William, married
George Parkin's second daughter, Maude, in 1911. William
Grant was appointed principal of UCC in 1918, the year
George Parkin Grant was born.

Good fortune seemed to follow men who married George
Parkin's daughters. One of Grant's uncles was Vincent
Massey, who married Maude Parkin's older sister, Alice.
Massey was briefly president of his family's farm-implement
company but is best known as Canada's first native-born
governor general. Massey also served as a politician, a diplo-
mat, and in 1950 was charged by Prime Minister Louis St.
Laurent with heading the Royal Commission on National
Development in the Arts, Letters, and Sciences. In 1915,
James Macdonnell was lucky enough to marry Maude's
younger sister, Marjorie Parkin. Macdonnell was an insur-

ance man who became one of the most respected Tory politicians of his generation, serving as a minister in John Diefenbaker's cabinet. On his father's side, Grant's aunt Allison
married the diplomat George Ignatieff, whom she met in
London during the Second World War. Their son, Michael
Ignatieff, is one of Canada's best-known public intellectuals.

As a result of these and other useful family connections,
George Grant's life gives the impression of considerable privilege, if not great wealth. Yet as William Christian notes in his
biography of Grant, while many of these figures attained
mid-century prominence in Canada, "it is easy to exaggerate
the eminence of the Masseys, Macdonnells, and Grants in the
1920s. Both George's grandfathers were of humble origins
and rose on their abilities alone. They attained prominent
educational positions, and these brought them into contact
with various levels of the élite both in Canada and in Great
Britain, but it did not make them rich."[12]

In 1916 William Grant had been seriously injured when he
was thrown from his horse while fighting in France. After
recovering for a year, he sailed back to Canada to a position
as principal of UCC. Almost a full year later, on 13 November 1918, George Parkin Grant was born in Toronto. After
spending most of his education at UCC, Grant went to
Queen's in 1936 to study history. He won a Rhodes scholarship and in 1940 went to Balliol College, Oxford, to study
law.

By this time Grant had become a committed Christian
pacifist, and he struggled with the burden of his family's
legacy of service to King and Country. With some fellow students he started a University Ambulance Unit, and then took
a job as an Air Raid Precautions officer, helping enforce
blackouts and doing first aid and rescue work while living in
a bomb shelter. In February 1941 Grant's shelter was
bombed and as many as three hundred people were killed.

On the brink of emotional and nervous exhaustion, Grant decided to join the navy but was rejected after failing a medical exam. He promptly disappeared and was completely out of touch with his family for a number of months. He finally resurfaced and made his way back to Canada to convalesce until the end of the war.

In 1945 Grant returned to Oxford to finish his Rhodes but switched from the study of law to a D.Phil in theology. While attending meetings of C.S. Lewis's Socratic Club, he met Sheila Allen, an English student and fellow pacifist. They were married in the spring of 1947, just as Grant was preparing to return to Canada to take up a position teaching philosophy at Dalhousie University in Halifax. He spent the next thirteen years there, during which time the Grants had six children. Dalhousie was a congenial place and the Grants had fallen in love with a property they had bought on Terrence Bay, but Grant felt the need to get back to Ontario, closer to the nerve centre of North American life. After a failed attempt to obtain an appointment to the newly created York University in Toronto, in 1961 he moved to the department of religion at McMaster University in Hamilton.

While Grant's first important book, *Philosophy in the Mass Age,* had been published in 1959, the sixties proved to be the decade that made his reputation. He became a national figure with the publication of *Lament for a Nation* in 1965. As we shall see, the book's underlying philosophical assumptions about the alienating and homogenizing effects of technology had a great deal in common with the counter-cultural critique of mass society that was gaining popularity amongst leftists and student radicals. Grant was also bitterly opposed to the war in Vietnam and for a while he was the darling of the student movement and the New Left, appearing frequently at teach-ins and protests on university campuses across the country. As William Christian observes, the relationship between Grant and the student movement was at best an alliance, not a "community of interest." Grant was a nationalist but he was also a conservative, and while the predominantly left-wing students might have been willing to focus more on Grant's argument that Canadian nationalists had to be socialists (and less on his religiosity), Grant disapproved of leftist utopianism and he could not abide some of the student movement's more socially disruptive tactics, like civil disobedience.[13]

Still, the encounter benefited both sides, in particular through Grant's relationship with the left-wing academic Gad Horowitz, with whom Grant co-hosted a weekly political talk show in Toronto in 1965. Horowitz coined the term "Red Tory" to describe conservatives who found themselves instinctively more drawn to socialists than to liberals, and socialists who found themselves more drawn to conservatives than to liberals. According to Horowitz, Canadian socialism emerges out of the "tory touch" brought to Canadian liberalism by the Loyalists.[14] Following the thought of Richard Hooker, this brand of conservatism believed in society as an organic entity, in which each part is responsible for the welfare of the whole. Grant claimed not to like the term, but it became a popular way of referring to a conservative tradition that favoured an interventionist state and rejected the economic continentalism of the Liberal party.

Lament was followed by the publication, in 1969, of a collection of essays called *Technology and Empire*, and later that same year Grant delivered the ninth Massey Lectures for CBC radio. An extended meditation on the thought of Friederich Nietszche, the lectures were broadcast under the title "Time as History." While on vacation in Barbados in May 1970, the Grants were in a serious automobile accident. Sheila suffered a broken shoulder and a concussion, while George broke a hand and a leg, and lost many of his teeth.

His recovery took up much of the next year, delaying the publication of *Time as History* until 1971.[15]

For the next decade, Grant was presented with numerous honourary degrees and entertained a succession of offers at competing universities across Canada. In 1980 he was finally brought back to Halifax by the president of Dalhousie, Henry Hicks, after having become disillusioned with his colleagues and with McMaster in general. He felt that the school had become overly concerned with 'research' devoted to serving the technocracy and had turned its back on the search for deeper truth. Yet the return to the Maritimes was not a great success, and Grant worked fitfully on what he hoped would be a grand academic project. A long-delayed set of essays was finally coaxed out of him by his friend and editor, the poet Dennis Lee, and published in 1986 as *Technology and Justice*. George Parkin Grant died of cancer on 27 September 1988.

For the contemporary reader, a certain confusion arises out of Grant's use of the terms "liberal" and "conservative" and his corresponding claim that in Canada, the Progressive Conservative party is the party of communitarianism and nationalism, while the Liberal party supports a more individualistic and continentalist pro-business agenda. This is confusing for a number of reasons. First, the use of the terms "liberal" and "conservative" in North America has become extremely convoluted and weighted with unfortunate connotations. Second, it will strike many readers that it gets Canada's current political alignment almost exactly backward.

The traditional left-right political spectrum puts "liberals" on the left, and "conservatives" on the right. This is inadequate, because it does not distinguish between the economic and social dimensions (see figure 1). A better way of graph-

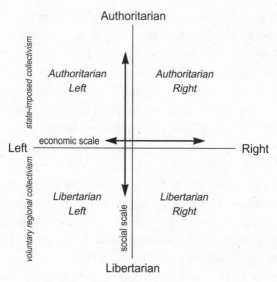

Figure 1   Political Compass

ing the political spectrum is to use two axes, one horizontal and one vertical, dividing the political space into four quadrants. The horizontal axis represents the economic dimension, with egalitarianism and collectivism on the left and pro-market liberal individualism on the right. The vertical axis represents the social dimension, with authoritarianism at the top and a rights-based libertarianism on the bottom. Thus, an authoritarian communist like Stalin appears in the top left of the north-west quadrant, while a free-market authoritarian like Augusto Pinochet of Chile will appear in the top right corner of the north-east quadrant.[16]

In Canada and the United States, it is now fashionable to speak of the conservative movement that began with the Reagan/Thatcher/Mulroney era in the 1980s and is now represented by George W. Bush's Republican Party in the United States. This obscures the fact that there are actually two movements involved. There is a "neo-liberal" group, which favours small government and tends to be economically quite liberal and socially libertarian, as well as a traditional conservative group, dominated by the religious right, which is socially authoritarian and is not necessarily opposed to high levels of public spending, especially on such things as the military. Compounding the problem is that, in the United States, "liberal" is used almost exclusively as a derogatory term and means something close to "socialist." In Canada and Britain, it retains its traditional associations with free market policies and individual liberties. This has given rise to the common usage "fiscal conservative but social liberal" to describe those who believe in low taxes, small government, and balanced budgets, while supporting many socially liberal causes such as gay rights and relaxed drug laws.

As we have seen, when Grant uses the term "conservative" he is referring to a British variant rooted in the pre-industrial thinking of Richard Hooker. This predominantly social conservatism privileges the interests of the community ahead of those of the individual, and emphasizes the public virtues of hierarchy, law and order, tradition, and organic change. This is a version of what philosophers call a "perfectionist" view of society, insofar as the public promotion of a certain conception of individual and collective human excellence is seen as one of the main functions of the state.

In contrast, the theoretical core of liberalism is the idea that the individual is the basic unit of value and the freedom of the individual takes priority over the interests of the community. Liberals take seriously what the philosopher John Rawls calls "the fact of pluralism" – that in any reasonably diverse society, people will inevitably hold competing and incompatible conceptions of what constitutes human excellence. For liberals, the function of the state is not to endorse or promote any specific version of the good life but to provide the conditions for the exercise of individual freedom.

This is why liberalism puts so much stock in individual rights and freedoms, in particular in the right to freedom of religion and conscience, freedom of speech, and freedom of association. In North America, liberalism has been heavily influenced by John Locke's notion of the individual as having innate rights to life, liberty, and property.

For the first hundred years or so after Confederation, Canada's main political parties more or less followed this philosophical division. That is, the Conservative party was more traditional, more nationalist, and more willing to use the power of the state to promote the collective good, while the Liberals were less keen on the British connection and more in favour of the free market and a contintentalist orientation favouring economic ties to the United States. As Kenneth McNaught put it in his review of *Lament* in *Saturday Night*, "it is now beyond doubt that the Conservatives, in recognizing the desperate need of a counter-balance to the American continental pull, have always been the more nationalist of the two major parties – and that their 'imperalism' was very largely an expression of that nationalism."[17]

We should not overstate the ideological differences between the two parties. To begin with, Canadian politics, especially at the federal level, has always been highly pragmatic. Throughout the country's history, both of the main political parties have shown themselves more than willing to abandon old positions, or even completely reverse themselves on major questions of policy. Second, we should not assume that the Loyalists flooded into Canada because of their commitment to a profound theory of political philosophy. North American conservatives and liberals are both heavily indebted to the thinking of John Locke. From a global perspective, Canada is a thoroughly North American nation, swimming comfortably in the Lockean end of the ideological pool. George Grant admitted as much and suggested that, philosophically, the Loyalists were at best "straight Locke with a dash of Anglicanism."[18]

Still, the presence of a tory strain of thinking has always exerted a considerable influence on Canadian politics (although that influence has been declining steadily since the 1960s). In particular, it has served to distinguish the various incarnations (see below) of the Canadian Conservative party from its American counterpart, the Republicans. As McNaught writes later in the same review of *Lament*, "Until very recently, the Tories have been much less afraid of the power of the state than have the Liberals," and their dislike of American republicanism does not arise out of mere anti-American prejudice. Rather, it is because "a society in which the profit motive is celebrated as the only valid criterion could hold no charm for genuine conservatives."[19] In an influential paper published in 1968, Gad Horowitz argues that while the Republican Party is almost monolithic in its Lockeanism, Canadian Conservatives "have something British and non-liberal about them. It is not simply their emphasis on loyalty to the crown and to the British connection, but also a touch of the authentic tory aura – traditionalism, elitism, the strong state, and so on. The Canadian Conservatives lack the American aura of rugged individualism."[20]

Matters have changed considerably in the forty years since the publication of *Lament for a Nation*. The first major shift occurred under Pierre Trudeau, when the Liberal party became less pro-business, less continentalist, and more nationalist, although it is hard to know how much of this was due to non-ideological factors. The late sixties and early seventies mark the high tide of English-Canadian nationalism, and the war in Vietnam and the growing sense that the United States was a society in a grave state of decline made appeals to Canadian nationalism a more viable political gambit. At the same time the oil crisis of the 1970s and the subsequent economic shocks led Trudeau to implement a number of statist controls over wages and prices, foreign investment (through FIRA, the Foreign Investment Review Agency), and energy policy (through the National Energy Program, or NEP). Philosophically, Trudeau was an arch anti-nationalist, but he used a strengthened bicultural and bilingual Canadian federation as a mechanism for containing Quebec nationalism.

One consequence of Diefenbaker's collapse was that the Conservative's power base shifted decisively to the West, to Alberta in particular. The party became increasingly fractious under Diefenbaker's successor, the Nova Scotian Robert Stanfield, as free-trading and populist westerners struggled with the more traditional tory elements in Ontario and the Maritimes. In 1983 the party united behind Brian Mulroney, in an anti-centrist coalition of pro-business Westerners and Quebec nationalists. Mulroney repealed both FIRA and the NEP and signed a free-trade agreement with the United States. The "free trade" election of 1988 cemented the status of the Conservatives as the party of capitalism, continentalism, and small, decentralised government, while John Turner's Liberals defended something akin to a "national policy" of protective tariffs and a strong central government.

As with Trudeau, it is hard to say how much of Mulroney's political agenda was ideological and how much was the usual mixture of ambition, opportunism, and political necessity. Ronald Reagan and Margaret Thatcher were busy pushing through fairly radical neo-liberal reforms in the United States and in Britain, and Mulroney certainly saw it as a bandwagon upon which it was in Canada's (and his own) interest to jump. Regardless, Mulroney's coalition cracked up soon afterward, and the old Progressive Conservative party was virtually destroyed in the election of 1993, replaced by the Bloc Québécois in Quebec and the Reform party in the West. The Reform Party was a mix of social conservatives, prairie populists, and pro-American continentalists, while the old Progressive Conservatives struggled on as a toryish Maritime rump. With the union of the Canadian Alliance (a successor to Reform) and the Progressive Conservatives in 2003, the new Conservative Party of Canada has become almost indistinguishable from the American Republican Party, itself composed of an unstable alliance of religious social conservatives and free-market liberals.

THE UNIVERSAL AND HOMOGENEOUS STATE

While the first three chapters of *Lament* are an examination of the fall of Diefenbaker's government, the book is not just (or even primarily) a political polemic. There are two distinct arguments braided into *Lament*'s seven short chapters, and while Grant clearly sees them as deeply connected, it is not obvious that there is any necessary conceptual relationship between them. It might be possible to accept the logic of one of the arguments, without having to accept the other.

The first argument is a sociological/political claim about the various threats Canada faces, given its status as a close-lying outpost of the American empire. To put it in a metaphor that has become part of our national self-understanding, the book is an exploration of the inevitable hazards of sleeping with an elephant. The second is an argument in political philosophy. Grant's claim here is that the emergence of liberalism and Marxism as the dominant political ideologies of the twentieth century has led to the obsolescence of conservatism as a viable political philosophy. Grant ties these arguments together by framing the entire discussion within a critique of the "ontology" of technological society and its role in erasing particular cultures and bringing about the "universal and homogenous state."[21] In *Lament*, Grant does not always make explicit the ways the two positions are supposed to be connected. That is partly because of the polemical nature of the book, but it is also because his thinking on these matters was still evolving. In many ways, it is helpful to read his later work, in particular the essays "In Defence of North America" and "Canadian Fate as Imperialism" in his 1969 book *Technology and Empire*, as completing the argument of *Lament for a Nation*.

Throughout almost all of his writing, Grant is exploring the contours of a single question: what does it mean to live in a technological society? Probing the structure of modernity was Grant's life work. It is not possible here to give a proper summary of the full depth of his thought, with all of its nuance and ambivalence – a quick look at the broad strokes of Grant's critique will have to suffice. The centre of Grant's position is a root-and-branch rejection of liberalism. In a somewhat syncretic critique that draws from the work of the philosophers Friederich Nietzsche and Martin Heidegger, the political theorist Leo Strauss, and the sociologist Jacques Ellul, Grant argues that there is a tight and interdependent relationship between liberalism as a political philosophy, its corresponding theory of justice, and the technological milieu of modernity.

It is important to note that Grant does not deny that some form of political liberty is a necessary element in the pursuit of excellence, but he finds liberalism inadequate as a *complete theory* of human good. For him, the decisive moment in liberal thinking came when western Europe rejected the traditional Aristotelian account of nature as a framework for understanding human excellence. On this traditional view, human beings were understood as "directed to a highest good under which all goods could be known in a hierarchy

of subordination and superordination."[22] The turning point
was when Locke, following Hobbes, substituted "the state of
nature for the createdness of nature as the primal truth."[23]
Whereas the Aristotelian view offered a positive theory of
human excellence, the Lockean view had only a negative theory of what was evil, namely death. For liberals, the good is
not given to us in virtue of who we are – as man *qua* man.
Rather, the good is something that we pursue according to
our privately held values. Because the state of nature is
potentially the scene of premature and painful death, the job
of the state becomes one of securing our life, liberty, and
property so that we might be free to pursue whatever conception of the good life we choose. For liberalism, the deepest human good *is* this freedom to choose, and pursue, our
own version of the good.

The corresponding theory of justice that emerges from this
view of the good is social contract theory, or *contractarianism*.
This theory holds that persons are primarily self-interested and
that a rational assessment of the best strategy for attaining the
maximization of their self-interest will lead them to agree to
abide by a set of coercive laws and institutions that preserve
the rights and freedoms of each, against all the rest. Grant
agrees with Nietzsche that the work of Immanuel Kant marks
the apotheosis of this line of thought.[24] For Kant, the highest
human good is dignity conferred through the autonomous
exercise of reason, from which it follows that "the best political regime is such as could be willed rationally by all its members. In this sense, consent becomes the very substance of the
best regime."[25] The political rights thus constituted are universal, applying to all humans equally, because "all human beings
are equal in the sense that they are all open to the highest
human end of willing the moral good."[26] Thus Kant tries to
ground his liberal account of equality in the abstract and eternal command of reason.

Grant follows Nietzsche in rejecting the "pseudo-universal-ism" of Kant's social contract, holding instead that Kant's liberal commitment to equality and justice is in fact supported by nothing more than convention and convenience. The entire liberal project of individual freedom is founded on nothing more substantial than "quality of life" considerations, which are, in the end, nihilistic.

What calls liberalism's bluff, according to Grant, is how it handles bioethical issues such as abortion and euthanasia, in particular in the 1973 Roe vs. Wade decision by the U.S. Supreme Court. In that decision the court affirmed that laws against abortion violate a constitutional right to privacy and that no state has the right to pass legislation that would prevent a woman from having an abortion in the first trimester of her pregnancy. For Grant, the heart of the decision is the assumption that what is at issue is the conflict between legislatures and the rights of "persons." Since the court has ruled that a fetus up to six months is not a "person," it has no status in the dispute. Grant argues that Roe v. Wade: "speaks modern liberalism in its pure contractual form: right prior to good; a foundational contract protecting individual rights; the neutrality of the state concerning moral values; social pluralism supported by and supporting this neutrality. Indeed the decision has been greeted as an example of the nobility of American contractarian institutions and political ideology, because the right of an individual 'person' is defended in the decision against the power of a majority in the legislature."[27]

For Grant, this decision raises a "poisoned chalice" to liberalism's lips. After all, if we can simply *decide* that fetuses are not persons, why can't we make the same decision about the very young, or the very old? Or criminals, the mentally ill, and those who are retarded? On what grounds would we make these decisions? What is so important, from the perspective of "personhood," about the ability to calculate or to

enter into and assent to contracts? For Grant, Roe v. Wade
throws these questions wide open by turning moral standing
("personhood") into a historically contingent concept that
will always be subject to change or revision. In Nietzsche's
terms, in abandoning an absolute standard of moral value we
have swept away the "horizon" against which our commitment to liberal egalitarianism could be justified: "The masses
blink and say: 'We are all equal. – Man is but man, before
God – we are all equal.' Before God! But now this God has
died."[28]

Grant sees Nietzsche as demonstrating the bankruptcy of
the liberal notion that we could have moral absolutism
within a secularized liberal framework based on the notion
of a social contract. By focusing on the idea of autonomous
"willing" that is at the heart of the liberal project, Nietzsche
unmasked the creed's essential nihilism. In turn, this nihilism
exposes us to technological tyranny. The connection works as
follows: because liberalism has the maximizing of human
freedom as its central good, anything that hinders the exercise of freedom is seen as an obstacle to be removed. This
has the effect of turning questions of ultimate value into matters of mere "convenience" or "quality of life." All reasoning
thus becomes "instrumental," in that we reason only about
means, not about ends. The self-interested, calculating individual who enters into the social contract is just as calculating when it comes to the pursuit of the good, but there is no
sense in which "reasoning" is about discovering the good by
getting it substantively right.

The problem with this liberal discourse of freedom and
values is that it is a language "fashioned in the same forge
together with the will to technology. To try to think them
separately is to move more deeply into their common origin."[29] This is because we live in an era in which the world
is conceived as indifferent to value, indifferent to our pur-

poses. We reason instrumentally about the pursuit of ends
that are given, but where do we discover our ends? Where do
our purposes come from? The consequence of taking seriously the liberal attachment to freedom is that "the content
of man's freedom becomes the actualizing of freedom for all
men. The purpose of action becomes the building of the universal and homogenous state – the society in which all men
are free and equal and increasingly able to realize their concrete individuality."[30]

For Grant, the moral discourse of freedom cannot be dis-
tinguished from our approach to technology, because once
the overriding moral imperative becomes the overcoming of
obstacles to individual freedom, we are necessarily thrust
into a technological society. Grant follows Jacques Ellul in
defining technology as "the totality of methods rationally
arrived at and having absolute efficiency (for a given stage of
development) in every field of human activity."[31] A technological society, then, is one that pursues the systematic appli-
cation of reason to the invention of tools and methods for
enhancing freedom by making all activity more efficient.

Liberalism thus encourages an instrumentalist attitude, in
which any technology is itself neutral insofar as it provides a
means to an end, but is not an end in itself. Technology is
just a set of instruments, made by human for the purpose of
achieving certain human goals. These technologies are "neutral instruments," in the sense that the morality of the goals
for which they are used is determined outside them. As an
exemplar of this "common-sense" view, Grant quotes a computer scientist, who declared that "the computer does not
impose on us the ways it should be used."[32]

The difficulty with this neutralist/instrumentalist approach
to technology is that it obscures the broader way in which
the world manifests itself to a technological society. On this
point, Grant follows Heidegger in seeing technology not as a

set of neutral instruments but as an entire "ontology." That is, technology is a way of apprehending the world, it is a mode of existence that transforms the way we know, think, and will. Modern technology as an ontology conceives of all of nature (including the human body) as a source of what Heidegger calls "standing reserve" – a source of energy or resources, stored in anticipation of future use. The essence of technology is that it constitutes a way of thinking (what Heidegger calls "enframing") in which the world is set before man, to be questioned, interrogated, and exploited. For Grant, technology is our "civilisational destiny" in that it embodies "all the fundamental presuppositions that the majority of human beings inherit in a civilization, and which are so taken for granted as the way things are that they are given an almost absolute status."[33]

This is why it is false to suppose that technology is neutral, that it does not embody a set of values that it imposes on us. As a relatively mundane example, Grant invites us to consider the effect of the automobile. In a sense, the car can be seen as a neutral instrument that does not impose on us the way it should be used, since the same automobile might serve as an ambulance, a taxi-cab, or a getaway car. Canadians adopted the automobile as the most efficient means for getting around, given our geographic circumstances and social purposes. Yet the automobile has been one of the central causes of Canada's political and economic integration with the United States.

In January 1965, as Grant was writing *Lament for a Nation*, Canada and the United States signed the Autopact, a limited free trade agreement that created a single North American market in automobiles and parts. This had the dual effect of both binding southern Ontario to the Michigan economy and also securing Canada's status as a branch plant economy. Our desire for the use of cars has led to our integration and

"our social homogenization with the people of the imperial heartland. This was not only because of the vast corporate structures
necessary for building and keeping in motion such automobiles, and
the direct and indirect political power of such corporations, but also
because any society with such vehicles tends to become like any
other society with the same. Seventy-five years ago somebody might
have said 'The automobile does not impose on us the ways it should
be used,' and who would have quarreled with that? Yet this would
have been a deluded representation of the automobile."34

   This is the point at which Grant's Nietzschean critique of
liberalism and Heideggerian critique of technology is hitched
to Ellul's sociological critique of mass society. Ellul agrees
with the Heidegger-Grant position that technology is not a
single tool or machine, or even a specific sphere of knowledge and production. Rather, it is our civilisational destiny,
which Ellul calls "la technique," through which the machine
and its values are fully integrated into society, creating the
"man-machine." He believes that technology will eventually
penetrate all aspects of society, from politics and economics
to education, medicine, and even our understanding of the
human body. Technology is such a powerful and value-laden
ideology that it will come to dominate our consciousness and
constrain our very sense of "freedom" and our sense of the
possibilities for thought and for action. It enslaves us even
while it appears to liberate, giving us a fragmented and
atomized society that is heavily dependent on the impersonal
and alienating institutions of mass society.
   This picture of technology as a universalizing and homogenizing force that dissolves all particularity remains extremely
influential. Criticisms of this sort are the bread and butter of
today's anti-globalisation activists, who worry that the cultural uniformity that has swept through North America will
soon extend to the rest of the planet. Non-western cultures

will be eradicated, absorbed into a nexus of technocratic liberalism and rampant consumer capitalism.

Indeed, much of Grant's writing anticipates the worries about the relationship between consumerism and citizenship that have become such a vital part of post-millennial public discourse.[35] For example, of the world of social-contract liberalism that he is critiquing in *English Speaking Justice*, he writes: "Can the calculating individual be a citizen in such a world, or does this account of human beings only lead to individuals concerned with consumption – above all entertainment and the orgasm and consumption?"[36] Of the pluralism with respect to the good that is held up as one of liberalism's virtues, he complains that "differences in the technological state are able to exist only in private activities: how we eat; how we mate; how we practice ceremonies. Some like pizza, some like steaks; some like girls, some like boys; some like synagogue, some like the mass. But we all do it in churches, motels, restaurants indistinguishable from the Atlantic to the Pacific."[37]

It is worth asking: what is so valuable about the particular as opposed to the universal, or heterogeneity as opposed to homogeneity? That is, why should we resist the emergence of a liberal society in which the pursuit of the good is relegated to the private realm? The simple answer is that as far as George Grant is concerned, liberalism would lead to the universal and homogenous state, and this state would be a tyranny. The argument for this is developed in what is perhaps Grant's most important scholarly paper, "Tyranny and Wisdom," which is included in the *Technology and Empire* collection.

In that essay, Grant mediates a dispute between Alexandre Kojève and Leo Strauss on the question of whether the emergence of a universal and homogenous state would be the end of human striving and struggle. Essentially a continuation of an ongoing dispute between Hegel and the Greeks, the argument takes place at a rather sophisticated level. The upshot, though, is that Grant sides with Strauss against Kojève in holding that the universal and homogenous state would be a tyranny and therefore would not entail the end of human struggle. Grant's contribution to the debate is to propose that the universal and homogenous state will emerge first under the guise of the liberal-technological empire spearheaded by the United States of America.[38]

In the universal and homogenous state, the sole object of loyalty is the calculating liberal individual. As Usuf Kumar writes: "Anything that is beyond the self is by definition a limitation on individuality, which in turn is a limitation on one's understanding of the self as freedom. Limitations on selfhood or individuality are encumbrances that must be removed if freedom is to be enjoyed to the fullest."[39] In contrast, what is valuable about particularity is that it provides a path away from the love of the self, toward the love of the good. The essence of particularity is what Grant calls "the love of one's own," and it is by loving our own that we move beyond the self and orient ourselves toward the love of something external. The highest end of man is to love the good, but the love of one's own is the necessary first step because it is what allows us to partake in a more universal good.

This way of understanding the deep structure of Grant's lament has an interesting corollary, which is that for Grant nationalism has a highly *instrumental* character. That is, there was never anything terribly special about Canada *per se*, except insofar as it might have provided a form of particularity in which we could love our own and thus learn to love the good. Grant was a supporter of a strong central government because he believed that national unity was the best hope for resisting the forces of Americanisation, not because he believed there was anything intrinsically worthwhile about Confederation as a whole.

Of course, the loss of one's own tradition will always be seen as tragic by those whose tradition has disappeared, although it isn't clear that what Canadians have lost is, in the grand scheme of things, all that big a deal. As Grant writes in the concluding passages of *Lament*, "Multitudes of human beings through the course of history have had to live when their only political allegiance was irretrievably lost. What was lost was often something far nobler than what Canadians have lost." Perhaps the best we can say about the disappearance of Canada is that if the American empire is indeed evolving into the tyranny of the universal and homogenous state, Canada's disappearance is "the removal of a minor barrier on the road to that tyranny" (94).

THE IMPOTENCE OF THE POLITICAL

Virtually every element of Grant's thought is controversial. At the very least, a proper critical discussion would address the following topics:

- Grant's somewhat crude and monotone interpretation of liberalism
- the nature of the relationship between technology and liberalism
- the alleged nihilism at the heart of liberalism
- the cogency of the slippery slope reasoning that equates tolerance of abortion with the denial of personhood to the elderly or the disabled
- the nature of the relationship between conservatism, socialism, and nationalism
- Grant's inadequately theorized account of nationalism

- Grant's unargued and undefended Platonism and religiosity

This is not the place to engage in such a thoroughgoing critique of Grant's thought, so we shall have to settle for looking a couple of issues that have been of constant concern since the earliest reviews of *Lament*. The first has to do with the apparent conflict between the political and the philosophical arguments in the book. The second concerns Grant's alleged pessimism, a charge which he resented and denied.

When *Lament* was first published in 1965, many reviewers picked up on what appeared to be a serious tension between the political argument that dominates the first three chapters and the philosophical point of view elaborated in the second half of the book. It is clear that Grant sees the fall of Diefenbaker as a political symptom of our deeper philosophical malaise, but, as Ramsay Cook argues, the two positions are actually at odds with one another. Throughout his writing, Grant praises a variety of Canadian conservative politicians, from Macdonald to Borden to (belatedly) Diefenbaker, while heaping scorn upon Liberals from Laurier to Pearson. This would indicate that Grant saw a conservative Canada as a possibility, its demise as a political failure. Yet Grant also writes in *Lament*: "British conservatism was already largely a spent force at the beginning of the 19th century when English-speaking Canadians were making a nation ... For all the fruitfulness of the British tradition in nineteenth century Canada, it did not provide any radically different approach to the questions of industrial civilization" (72–3).In order to lament the death of a nation it must first have lived, but Grant suggests that it was in fact stillborn. In which case it is not American control and Liberal perfidy that destroyed Canada but the age of progress.[40]

Grant himself encouraged this reading of his book. In the introduction to the 1970 Carleton Library edition of *Lament*, he repeated the assertion that British conservatism was itself largely beaten in Britain by the time it was inherited by Canadians, and "The twentieth century was not a period in which it was wise to rely on British traditions as counter-attractions to the American dream. Yet these were what we had" (lxxiv). Hence, it was wrong of people to interpret the book as a lament for the passing of the British dream for Canada. It was, rather, "a lament for the romanticism of the original dream" (lxxiv). Ramsey Cook points out that this tension is only resolved in Grant's later work, when his thesis about technology is pushed through to its logical, fully pessimistic conclusion. Particularly relevant are the essays in *Technology and Empire*, where the argument about the fundamental unity of liberalism, technology, and empire is more fully developed. Yet this argument resolves the tension between the political and the philosophical in Grant's thought only by adopting a form of technological determinism that makes politics impotent.

Technological determinism is the thesis that technology evolves according to its own internal logic and laws and is therefore a highly autonomous system that determines the nature of other social institutions. It is a variation on the Marxian base-superstructure analysis of society, in which the economic "base" determines the social "superstructure," particularly the legal and political institutions of the state. The difference is that while Marx focused on a society's given means of production, the technological determinist emphasizes the nature of its technological development.

One consequence of this sort of thinking is that it prevents us from taking political institutions — and the differences between them — seriously. In chapter 6 of *Lament*, Grant muses about what might keep Canada independent from the

United States: "The Laurentian Shield and the Eskimos?
British tradition has provided us with certain political and
legal institutions, some of which are better than their American counterparts. Our parliamentary and judicial institutions
may be preferable to the American system, but there is no
deep division of principle. Certainly none of the differences
between the two sets of institutions are sufficiently important
to provide the basis for an alternative culture on the northern
half of the continent" (72).

What is curious about this is that a significant element of
the Loyalist motivation for coming to Canada in the first
place was a preference for the parliamentary form of government. The Loyalists saw republicanism and its reliance on
popular sovereignty as a genuine threat to the liberties
enshrined in the British form of constitutional monarchy.
Furthermore, it has been widely argued that the differences
in the political cultures of Canada and the United States are,
to a large extent, the result of the operation of, and socializa-
tion under, different institutions. This is why the journalist
David Warren – a self-described "disciple" of Grant's – suggests that a Canadian nationalist should be concerned primarily with the preservation of Canadian political institutions, especially the fusion of the executive and the legislative
branches.

The American congressional system has a genuine separa-
tion of powers, in which the head of the executive branch
(the president) and the members of the bicameral legislature
are elected separately, with each having a share of the executive and legislative power. In Canada, only the members of
the House of Commons are elected, and it is from this body
that the members of the executive (the prime minister and
Cabinet) are chosen. The Canadian Senate is appointed and
wields relatively little political power. This fusion of the executive and legislative powers is known as government through

"the Crown-in-Parliament." When the government enjoys the support of the majority of the House of Commons, it allows for much for effective and decisive action by the executive without the vote-buying and "horse trading" that character-izes much of American federal politics. According to Warren, "More than anything in the attic, this is what distinguishes us from the Republicans to the south: the essentially unicam-eral nature of our (ceremonially bicameral) parliament."[41]

Yet once you adopt Grant's technological determinism, it becomes hard to take seriously these sorts of "merely institu-tional" differences. Politics becomes epiphenomenal, its ulti-mate character dictated by the underlying technological real-ity. That is why Grant dismissed liberalism as the "civil theology" of technological society, and why he followed Hei-degger in claiming that there were no important differences between communism, Nazism, and the United States of America, since all three were equally committed to the imper-atives of progress through technological reason.[42]

For many people, even those highly sympathetic to Grant's overall argument, this is just too crude a picture of the world. In his 1965 review of *Lament*, Gad Horowitz objected to Grant's assertion that a society could not adopt a progressive approach to technology and still remain un-Americanised in its political ideology and social structure. Must countries as diverse as Sweden, Japan, and Australia all end up as replicas of America, outposts of the empire? Surely not, said Horowitz: a conservative like Grant should realize that "Americanization does not work on a *tabula rasa*. The past cannot be entirely erased."[43] In a similar vein, Arthur Kroker argues that the signal failure of Grant's philosophy is that it cannot be translated into political action. His diagno-sis of the modern predicament ends with a lament for what has been lost instead of a prescription for what can be saved. Ultimately, Grant simply retreats into a strongly held, but completely unargued, religiosity, which Kroker calls Grant's "panic remembrance" of the safety of natural law.[44]

For Horowitz, Kroker, and plenty of other Canadian nationalists, Grant's biggest failure is his unwillingness to even attempt the difficult but essential task of reconciling twentieth-century technology with twentieth-century justice. Behind this failure lies Grant's overwhelming and unsurmountable pessimism, which sucks the life out of political hope while advocating a retreat into the cynical smugness of despair. As Horowitz points out, nothing – not even philosophy – can tell us what is inevitable, until it actually happens. Until then, there is no reason not to fight because there is "a difference between going down fighting and going down smirking. But the danger of Grant's pessimism is that it encourages smirking rather than fighting. Why give up the fight unless you know for certain that it is lost. Grant's pessimism and determinism exude death."[45]

ON PESSIMISM

Was George Grant a pessimist? It is difficult to see how one could conclude otherwise. Throughout his writing, he freely indulged in the language of inevitability, of fate, of Canada's "destiny." He was certain of the nature of that fate, which was to be absorbed first into the American technological empire, then into the universal and homogenous state. Finally, while *Lament* ends on a slightly ambiguous note as to whether the disappearance of Canada would be, ultimately, a bad thing, Grant's subsequent work made it clear that the universal and homogenous state would be a tyranny, which would cut humans off from the loving of one's own that is a precursor to loving the good. All in all, Grant does not offer the sympathetic reader much to be optimistic about.

In the opening lines of "Canadian Fate and Imperialism" Grant writes: "To use the language of fate is to assert that all human beings come into a world they did not choose and live their lives within a universe they did not make."[46] This way of putting it says nothing about necessity, and to speak of Canada's fate in such terms is to point out the obvious, that the Canadian question has always been tied up with its relationship to empire, first as a British colony and then as an American branch-plant. That is the context in which Canada's national destiny must inevitably play out. But in many other places Grant makes far stronger claims about Canada's fate as being inevitable absorption by the United States. What distinguishes Grant from the liberal progressives is that while they see it as both necessary and good that Canada should disappear, Grant sees it as necessary and bad. The claim that something is both bad and inevitable would certainly seem to qualify as "pessimistic."

Grant's defense against the charge of pessimism consists of three related arguments. First, throughout his life he maintained that "it always matters what each of us does" (98). In the most practical sense, he held this to mean that even when caught up in powerful historical forces, human actions can always make a difference. For example, Grant points out that even while Canadian corporations were profiteering from the war in Vietnam, it was worth taking steps to preserve what remained of our sovereignty. "However disgraceful has been our complicity in the Vietnam War, however disgusting the wealth we have made from munitions for that war, one must still be glad that Canadian forces are not fighting there. This is due to what little sovereignty we still possess."[47] Yet as William Christian observes, this is at best a highly restricted and tactical sort of nationalism, committed only to the proposition that the only question about the inevitable is whether it occurs more or less quickly.[48] As a practical guide for achieving lasting political change, it is worthless.

To understand how Grant could lament the loss of the very possibility of doing politics,[49] yet also claim that it always matters what each of us does, it is important to see that he means that it "matters" in a very personal and spiritual sense. As Sheila Grant writes in her postscript to the 1997 edition of *Lament*, "It matters not only because of the possible results of our actions but because we are all free to turn towards good action, however difficult that choice may be. For one who believes, as [George] Grant did, that the spiritual life is open to all, pessimism is not an option" (98). This is not much different from something Grant wrote to a friend in 1961: "Nationalism is not a great thing in the Christian life."[50]

Lurking behind all of this is the conviction that a theist can't really be a pessimist, since God's grace is always at hand, if only we have the courage to open ourselves up to it. Because of this, Grant didn't like the language of pessimism and optimism applied to mere politics. He preferred to reserve it for the theological realm, as a way of characterizing our judgments in light of eternity and the divine. More specifically, he followed the philosopher Gottfried Leibniz in using the words "optimistic" and "pessimistic" to describe our convictions about the nature of the cosmos taken as a whole.[51] Leibniz is probably the most well-known philosophical "optimist," notorious for claiming that this is the best of all possible worlds. He was ridiculed for this by Voltaire in *Candide*, but Voltaire's was a crude reading of what is one of the most sophisticated and rational philosophical systems ever developed. Grant followed a broadly Leibnizian line in holding that any question of pessimism or optimism must be answered in light of the recognition that there is a divine order to the cosmos, whose ulti-

mate goodness is not impugned by the occurrence of particular evils.

But this does not clear Grant of the charge that he is a
pessimist. After all, his critics have never accused him of
being a pessimist in the Leibnizian sense. Rather, they have
always accused him of being a mundane political pessimist.
For him to answer a political charge with an appeal to metaphysical doctrine is somewhat disingenuous and only
changes the subject. And there is no question that he was a
thoroughgoing pessimist about political matters. No optimist could have written the lines that conclude "Canadian
Fate and Imperialism":

"But what lies behind the small practical question of Canadian
nationalism is the larger context of the fate of western civilization. By that fate I mean not merely the relations of our massive
empire to the rest of the world, but even more the kind of existence which is becoming universal in advanced technological societies. What is worth doing in this barren twilight is the incredibly
difficult question."[52]

POST-MODERN CANADA

Given that George Grant *was* pessimistic about the future of
Canada (and, probably, the future of the western world), it is
worth concluding with a look at the state of Canadian
nationalism at the turn of the millennium. In many ways, it
would appear that Canadian nationalism is weaker now than
it has ever been, having been almost completely marginalized
by the combined forces of Quebec nationalism, entrenched
regionalism, and North American economic integration. [53]
This would appear to vindicate the closing paragraph of
chapter 6 of *Lament*, where Grant writes: "Canada has

ceased to be a nation, but its formal political existence will
not end quickly. Our social and economic blending into the
empire will continue apace, but political union will probably
be delayed. Some international catastrophe or great shift of
power might speed up this process. Its slowness does not
depend only on the fact that large numbers of Canadians do
not want it, but also on sheer lethargy" (85).

This is a passage that, in light of recent events, seems
almost freakishly prescient. By the turn of the millennium, it
struck many political observers that Grant's predictions of
Canada's ultimate demise were finally on the verge of coming
true. In the wake of NAFTA, continental economic integration
was proceeding comfortably and the rumblings of continentalism grew increasingly hard to ignore, thanks in no small
part to the extremely pro-American agenda of a new national
newspaper, *The National Post*, which Conrad Black launched
in 1998. Then terrorists struck the Pentagon and the World
Trade Center on September 11, 2001.

The Canadian chattering classes quickly concluded that
Canada had become obsolete overnight. The twin require-
ments of economic and physical security meant that the
Americans would no longer indulge the fantasies of Canadian nationalists and that Ottawa was now little more than a
puppet regime of Washington. For example, in the *Toronto
Star*, columnist Richard Gwyn announced that Canada had
entered the "virtual sovereignty" phase of its existence.[54]
Meanwhile, the continentalist agenda became more pressing.
There were renewed calls for a sort of "NAFTA-plus" agreement, built around some "big idea" or "grand bargain" in
which Canada would transfer a great deal of its sovereignty
to the United States in exchange for economic security.[55] Elements of the "big idea" package included proposals for a
customs union, integrated security agencies, and dollariza-
tion. Wrapping it all in the Grantian language of historical

inevitability, Michael Bliss published a three-part series in the *National Post* on Canadian identity, in which he argued that Canada's ongoing attempts at nation-building had been a failure and that the country ought to give serious thought to joining the United States of America.[56] For Canadian nationalists, the eighteen months after September 11 were very dark times, to the point where it often seemed that, this time, the centre could not hold.

But weak and marginal as it is, Canadian nationalism is also tenacious, and an argument could be made that it is stronger now than it has been in a quarter century. The country seemed to get a genuine boost of self-confidence from the gold medals in men's and women's hockey at the Salt Lake City Olympics in 2002, and Prime Minister Jean Chrétien's decision to keep Canada out of the invasion of Iraq in March 2003 was a more forceful assertion of Canadian military independence than Diefenbaker's waffling on the Bomarc missiles. This newly won national confidence did not go unnoticed: the cover story of the September 27, 2003 edition of *The Economist* was called "Canada's New Spirit," and featured a photograph of a moose wearing sunglasses.

It is doubtful that Grant would be much heartened by the character of this nationalism. More than likely, he would be astonished at its prevalence and disappointed at its character. Far from the orderly, organic, hierarchical conservatism that Grant assumed was the necessary heart of the Canadian national project, the current brand of Canadian nationalism is the exact opposite, an almost gleefully individualistic and non-deferential hyper-cosmopolitanism.

This nationalism began in the 1970s as a combination of the political and the literary. Many Canadians were attracted to Pierre Trudeau's internationalism and his social libertarianism, characterized by his famous remark that "the state has no business in the nation's bedrooms."[57] Around the same time, an English-Canadian literary sensibility was developing, thanks in large part to Margaret Atwood's book *Survival*. In that book Atwood argued that every country has "a single unifying and informing symbol at its core." The symbol acts as a centre of narrative gravity, providing a focus for the collective identity that "holds the country together and helps the people cooperate for common ends." She suggested, for example, that England's symbol was The Island, serving as a metaphor for the self-contained monarchical Body Politic. In North America, the symbol in the USA is The Frontier, "a line that is always expanding, taking in or 'conquering' ever-fresh virgin territory (be it The West, the rest of the world, outer space, Poverty, or The Regions of the Mind.)" Upon Canada, Atwood bestowed the symbol "Survival." For the earliest explorers, that meant survival in the meanest and most basic physical sense, but in later Canadian writing survival came to refer to more spiritual obstacles. In Atwood's hands, survival became a struggle against colonial oppression, with Canada as the innocent virgin fighting off the virile advances of the masculine American empire.[58] Through Atwood, Canadian nationalism was restated in the cosmopolitan and emancipatory vocabulary of 1970s feminism and post-colonial theory.[59]

As a historical thesis, this is certainly false. "Survival" is not a national symbol that either of Grant's grandfathers would have found remotely comprehensible, since they were fond of empire and more apt to see themselves as the colonizers, not the colonized. Atwood was right to draw attention to the mythological relationship Canadians have developed with the land, but for the first 100 years of the country's existence it was a mythology expressed in the language of technology, domination, and development.[60] When the myth of the land was paired with fashionable nineteenth-century theories about the role of the northern climate in

developing national character, you had the makings of a
muscular and expansionist national symbol. In 1954, it was
still possible for the socialist law professor and poet F.R.
Scott to write a poem called "Laurentian Shield," with this
last stanza:

> But a deeper note is sounding, heard in the mines,
> The scattered camps and the mills, a language of life,
> And what will be written in the full culture of occupation
> Will come, presently, tomorrow,
> From millions whose hands can turn this rock into
> children.[61]

Nevertheless, there is no disputing that the portrayal of
Canada as yin to the American yang has been an enormously
successful statement of Canada's contemporary self-understanding. For example, in his 1995 book *Nationalism Without Walls*, Richard Gwyn states, without argument or support, that we can cut through all the verbiage over Canadian
identity by noting that Canada represents "the feminine principle in North America."[62]

Today, there are various strains of this nationalism, from
the literary nationalism of the post-Atwood CanLit establishment[63] to the McLuhanesque technological nationalism of
B.W. Powe. The best general characterization of this movement is the phrase "post-modern nationalism," a usage that
was popularized in the early 1990s by the journalist Robert
Fulford and the literary theorist Linda Hutcheon.[64] The idea,
as Gwyn writes, is that Canada is the world's first "postmodern nation," in the sense that its statehood is not a consequence of typically modern factors such as shared language, ethnicity, and history. Instead, Canada has steadily
evolved into an anti-nation, characterized by "imperma-
nence, mutability, plasticity, and fragility. Canada is no

longer a nation-state but a postmodern something. Canadians are 'charting new territory' without knowing what or
where it is."[65] Similarly, B.W. Powe argues that Canada is a
"communication state," held together by nothing more than
a loose commitment to keeping the conversation going.
Canada is now a state-in-progress, a constant becoming with
no stable identity. [66]

A controversial statement of this position is found in the
2003 book *Fire and Ice* by the pollster Michael Adams. For
ten years, Adams tracked changes in "social values" in both
Canada and the United States. Social values are the various
beliefs and preferences people have of what constitutes the
good life, such as community involvement, tolerance, and
religiosity. Adams' results are interesting. He argues that
since 1992 social values between the two countries have
diverged in significant ways and that the long-term trend
points to increasing divergence. Both countries are trending
to move away from traditional values and are becoming less
deferential to authority and more individualistic. But while
Canadians are moving toward cosmopolitan values associated with idealism and personal self-fulfillment (e.g., creativity, tolerance, and cultural sampling), Americans are moving
away en masse from the trends associated with civic engage-
ment and social and ecological concern. Instead, Americans
are retrenching, becoming paranoid and isolated in an
increasingly Hobbesian society in which it is the war of all
against all. Says Adams, "What is remarkable about social
change in America is the society's absolute failure – or refusal
– to postmodernize. Nothing is more striking than the country's wholesale retreat from the idealism and fulfillment side
of the map."[67]

Fire and Ice has proven quite popular among nationalists
because it appears to vindicate precisely the sort of postmodern nationalism that has been incubating in Canada since the

early 1970s. Adams' work is not without its critics though, and even if his results are sound it is not obvious that empirical data on converging versus diverging values is the right place for a nationalist to hang her coat. While this is not the place to debate these issues, I can finish with a few brief points.

First, this Canadian cosmopolitan nationalism is surely a position about which Grant would have had little nice to say. He would have disliked the permissiveness, secularism, and individualism of twenty-first-century Canadian society. He may have expected it, but he wouldn't have liked it, and he wouldn't have seen it as recognizably Canadian. If anything, Grant would find himself in general sympathy with the American religious right, which is fighting to preserve the very values that Grant saw as essential to Canadian nation-hood. It is no small irony that American religious leaders such as Pat Buchanan despise Canadians for becoming, with respect to social progressiveness, more American than the Americans.

But it is not just that Grant would have disliked the idea of Canada as a postmodern nation. He would have seen it as incoherent. As far as he was concerned, the liberal principles at the heart of this postmodern politics should have caused Canada to disappear, since national particularity is not com-patible with liberalism. The problem here is that Grant had a very crude understanding of nationalism, though to some extent that is not his fault. The study of nationalism and how it can be accommodated within the framework of liberal theory was very underdeveloped until the 1990s, when the field exploded. To a large extent, this development was a much-needed response to the resurgence in nationalism in Europe after the fall of the Berlin Wall, and Grant can cer-tainly be forgiven for missing out on the great work that was done after he died in 1988.

Yet as early as 1970 Ramsey Cook was chiding Grant for his "naïve" thoughts about modern nationalism. Cook points out that, in direct contradiction to what Grant was arguing, "modern nationalism, the ethos of progress, and the ideology of liberalism, appeared almost coincidentally." He suggests that this was no accident, since the notion of national self-determination provides a sense of purpose and direction for a society undergoing rapid change. It is unsurprising, then, to see that the world's most technologically advanced societies – Japan and the United States – are also the most nationalistic.[68]

In the end, it would appear that Grant was simply wrong. The impossibility of conservatism in Canada is just that: the impossibility of a tory form of social conservatism in a multicultural and pluralistic society. Some might find that worth lamenting, but from it nothing else follows – not the end of Canada, and certainly not the technological tyranny of the universal and homogeneous state.

Yet George Grant's *Lament for a Nation* is more than just a period piece, and it remains vital reading for even the most casual student of Canada. Even if we reject his technological determinism, his analysis of Canada's underlying political dynamic is still relevant, indeed occasionally freakishly prescient. As Grant shows, the most important faultline in Canadian federal politics is not the one between the political left and right, nor between the French and the English, but between those who favour an independent Canada and those who desire ever closer continental integration. To the extent that that is true, Grant's characterization of the Liberals as the party that demands only that "they have personal charge of the government while our sovereignty disappears," is, if anything, more brutally accurate today than it was in 1965. Finally, anyone trying to understand the ongoing failure of the Canadian conservative movement to provide a coherent and stable alternative to the Liberals would do well to study Grant's analysis of the career and character of John Diefenbaker.

For these reasons and many others, we should continue to read *Lament for a Nation*. Canada may, indeed, be doomed. It could split apart, with its various fragments going their own way or perhaps suing for admittance to the American union. Or the entire country could eventually become subsumed into a greater North American political entity. Either of these scenarios might come to pass, but perhaps neither of them will. Regardless, we won't find any answers in philosophy. Canada's fate, in the early years of the twenty-first century, is no more and no less certain than it was on the first of July 1867, when the long-dreamt Dominion became a reality. Canada was born on that day and it lives still, its people free to shape their country's destiny as best they can, under the unavoidable circumstances.

NOTES

This introduction was written while I was a post-doctoral fellow at the Centre de Recherche de l'Ethique de l'Université de Montréal (CREUM). Thanks are due to my fellow CREUMiens for comments and suggestions, especially to Colin Macleod, Avigail Eisenberg, Wayne Norman, and Joseph Heath.

1 Emberly, Peter C., "Forward," in Grant, George, *Lament for a Nation* (Montreal: McGill-Queen's University Press, 1997), lxxviii.
2 More accurately, the Statute of Westminster granted full legal freedom *except in those areas in which the Dominions desired to remain subordinate*. In Canada, the federal and provincial governments were not able to come to an agreement on a domestic amending formula for the constitution, so the amendment of the BNA Act was exempted from the provisions of the Statute. It was not until Patriation in 1982 that Canada took domestic control over the amendment of its own constitution.

3 Speech quoted in Newman, Peter C., *Renegade in Power: The Diefenbaker Years* (Toronto: McClelland and Stewart, 1973), 51.

4 All page references in parentheses are to the present edition of *Lament for a Nation*.

5 Newman, *Renegade in Power*, xix.

6 It is interesting to note the frequency with which "indecisive" recurs as a lamentable character trait of Canadian prime ministers. Macdonald was known as "Old Tomorrow," while Mackenzie King was eulogized by the poet F.R. Scott as having taught us to "Do nothing by halves/Which can be done by quarters." Jean Chrétien was later pegged by the media as the living embodiment of King's spirit of "Postpone, postpone, abstain," and his successor, Paul Martin, has been gleefully tagged with the title "Mr. Dithers." George Grant's observation that "decisiveness" is identified with doing what the Americans want applies as much to Paul Martin's 2005 decision to not participate in the U.S. Ballistic Missile Defence program as it does to Diefenbaker's actions during the Defence Crisis.

7 This is the conclusion Mordecai Richler drew in his 1965 review of *Lament*. He wrote that the upshot of Canadian nationalism was "to turn pinched backs on the most exciting events on the continent and to be a party to one of the most foolish, unnecessary, and artificial of frontiers." Richler, Mordecai, "The Declaration of Dependence," *Bookweek*, October 31, 1965.

8 Variations of this position are widespread in the literature. Harold Innis referred to Canada as "the storm centre of modernity," while the Innisian communications theorist B.W. Powe has described Canada as "the laboratory of the western world," where the effects of technology will be felt first. Powe, B.W., *A Tremendous Canada of Light* (Toronto: Coach House, 1993).

9 Grant, *Technology and Empire* (Toronto: Anansi, 1969), 64.

10 The Constitutional Act, 1791, reorganized British North America in the wake of the American Revolution and the influx of Loyalists into the northern colonies. The Act created Upper and Lower Canada as distinct provinces, a step that led, ultimately, to Confederation.

11 Taylor, Charles, *Radical Tories: The Conservative Tradition in Canada* (Toronto: Anansi, 1982), 148.

12 Christian, William, *George Grant: A Biography* (Toronto: University of Toronto Press, 1993), 10.

13 Ibid.

14 Horowitz, Gad, *Canadian Labour in Politics* (Toronto: University of Toronto Press, 1968), 10.

15 Christian, *George Grant*, 285.

16 For a graphic representation (and a quiz) visit *www.politicalcompass.org*

17 McNaught, Kenneth, "National Affairs," *Saturday Night*, August 1965, 7.

18 Grant, *Technology and Empire*, 68.

19 McNaught, "National Affairs," 9.

20 Horowitz, *Canadian Labour in Politics*, 20.

21 This paragraph draws on the scheme laid out in Crook, R.K., "Modernization and Nostalgia: A Note on the Sociology of Pessimism," review of *Lament for a Nation, Queen's Quarterly* 73 (1966): 269–84. This is not to endorse Crook's conclusions.

22 Grant, George, *English-Speaking Justice* (Notre Dame: University of Notre Dame Press, 1985), 17

23 Ibid., 16.

24 Philosophers distinguish between *contractarianism*, which derives from Hobbes and focuses on individual self-interest, and *contractualism*, which is Kantian and focuses on the respect owed to persons. Grant does not recognize this distinction and tends to conflate the various views held by Hobbes, Locke, and Kant.

25 Grant, *English-Speaking Justice*, 27.

26 Ibid.

27 Ibid., 70.

28 Ibid., 77.

29 Grant, George, "In Defence of North America," *Technology and Empire* (Toronto: Anansi, 1969), 32.

30 Ibid., 33.

31 Jacques Ellul, quoted in Grant, *Technology and Empire*, 113.

32 Grant, *Technology and Justice* (Toronto: Anansi, 1986), 19. See also Heidegger, Martin, *The Question Concerning Technology and Other Essays* (New York: Harper Perennial, 1982).

33 Grant, *Technology and Justice*, 22.

34 Ibid., 24–5.

35 For a critical examination, see Heath, Joseph, and Andrew Potter, *The Rebel Sell: Why the Culture Can't Be Jammed* (Toronto: HarperCollins, 2004).

36 Grant, *English-Speaking Justice*, 41.

37 Grant, *Technology and Empire*, 26.

38 Umar, Usuf K. "The Philosophical Context of George Grant's Political Thought," in *George Grant and the Future of Canada* (Calgary: University of Calgary Press, 1992), 9.

39 Ibid., 9.

40 Cook, Ramsey, "Loyalism, Technology, and Canada's Fate," *Journal of Canadian Studies* 5 (1970): 56.

41 Warren, David, "On George Grant's Nationalism,"in Peter C. Emberly, ed., *By Loving Our Own* (Ottawa: Carleton University Press, 1990), 70.

42 Gillespie, Michael Allan "George Grant and the Tradition of Political Philosophy," in Emberly, *By Loving Our Own*, 126.

43 Horowitz, Gad, "Tories, Socialists, and the Demise of Canada," *Canadian Dimension* (1965): 15.

44 Kroker, Arthur, *Technology and the Canadian Mind*, (Montreal: New World Perspectives, 1985), 50.

45 Horowitz, "Tories, Socialists, and the Demise of Canada," 15.

46 Grant, *Technology and Empire*, 63.

47 Ibid., 77.

48 Christian, *George Grant*, 251.

49 Ibid., 252.

50 Ibid.

51 Grant, *Technology and Empire*, 63.

52 Ibid., 78.

53 See for example Savoie, Donald J., "All Things Canadian Are Now Regional," *Journal of Canadian Studies* 35, 1 (2000).

54 Gwyn, Richard, "We Must Accept the Inevitable," *Toronto Star*, Sept 30, 2001, A.13

55 See for example: Gotlieb, Allan, "A Grand Bargain with the U.S.," *The National Post*, March 5, 2003; Dobson, Wendy, "Shaping the Future of the North American Economic Space," C.D. Howe Institute, *Commentary* 162 (April 2002).

56 Bliss, Michael, "The Identity Trilogy," *The National Post*, January 13–15, 2003.

57 This is usually misquoted as "the state has no business in the bedrooms of the nation."

58 Atwood, Margaret, *Survival: A Thematic Guide to Canadian Literature* (Toronto: Anansi, 1972), 31–2.

59 See David Warren's contribution in Emberly, *By Loving Our Own*, 69.

60 See Charland, Maurice, "Technological Nationalism," *Canadian Journal of Political and Social Theory* 10, 1–2 (1986): 196–220.

61 Scott, F.R., *The Collected Poems of F.R. Scott*, (Toronto: McClelland and Stewart, 1981), 58. It is useful to contrast this defunct form of Canadian nationalism with the preamble to the Sovereignty Bill introduced into the Quebec legislature by the Parti Québécois in 1995. The preamble opens with the following lines: "The time has come to reap the fields of history. The time has come at last to harvest what has been sown for us by four hundred years of men and women and courage, rooted in the soil and now returned to it. The time has come for us, tomorrow's ancestors, to make ready for our descendants harvests that are worthy of the labours of the past. May our toil be worthy of them, may they gather us together at last."

62 Gwyn, Richard, *Nationalism Without Walls*, (Toronto: McLelland and Stewart, 1995). 49. In making this claim, Gwyn of course has to ignore the status of hockey as an integral element of the Canadian identity.

63 For an argument that this Toronto-centric literary nationalism is fundamentally continentalist, see Henighan, Stephen, *When Words Deny the World: The Reshaping of Canadian Writing*, (Erin, ON: Porcupine's Quill, 2002)

64 See Fulford's essay "A Postmodern Dominion" in William Kaplan, ed., *Belonging: The Meaning and Future of Canadian Citizenship* (Montreal: McGill-Queen's University Press, 1993), and Hutcheon, Linda, "As Canadian as Possible... Under the Circumstances," in Lynch, Gerald, and Rampton, David, eds., *The Canadian Essay*. (Toronto: Copp Clark Pitman, 1991).

65 Gwyn, *Nationalism Without Walls*, 248.

66 Powe, *A Tremendous Canada of Light*.

67 Adams, Michael, *Fire and Ice: The United States, Canada, and the Myth of Converging Values*, (Toronto: Penguin, 2003), 44–5.

68 Cook, "Loyalism, Technology, and Canada's Fate," 58.

Introduction to the Carleton Library Edition

GEORGE GRANT

THE CARLETON LIBRARY HAS KINDLY suggested the reissuing
of this book – 'kindly' because it is a book written out of
particular events, and one therefore in which any general
truths arise in the context of circumstances eight years old. It
is a disadvantage these days for any general thesis to be tied
to past events, because eight years seems more than a generation. Our memories are killed in the flickering images of the
media, and the seeming intensity of events. There is weak-
ened in us the simplest form of that activity of re-collection
which Plato knew to be the chief means to wisdom.

It may be well therefore to preface a new edition by asking
the question: how do we stand in 1970 compared with
1963? The central problem for nationalism in English-speaking Canada has always been: in what ways and for what reasons do we have the power and the desire to maintain some
independence of the American empire? (It would be imperti-
nent indeed to define what is the chief problem for French-
speaking nationalism.) On the surface it is certainly much
easier in 1970 than it was in 1963 for Canadians not to want
to be swallowed by the U.S. The years of the Vietnam war
have been an exposition (a veritable Expo) of the American
empire. It does not take much intelligence or patriotism to be
glad that one's children are not drafted for that war. The
mainland of that empire no longer seems so rewarding a
place to live. Even the Canadian bourgeoisie can see the

perhaps unresolvable racial conflict, the expansion and decay
of its cities, the increase of military influence in constitutional
life, the breakdown between the generations, the effects of a
century of environmental spoliation, etc. etc. In 1963 we
could swim or go fishing in Lake Erie without cleaning off
the excrement. Today nobody can forget Cleveland. Such
events make possible a nationalist appeal to many Canadian
voters. And underlying the particular difficulties of the
empire is the deeper anxiety as to the very possibility of the
good life in civilization ruled by the spirit of dynamic technique. This spectre is naturally enough glimpsed most often
in the U.S.A. Eight years ago such anxiety was considered
nutty reaction; today it stalks the public world.

   During the missile crisis of 1963, the U.S.A. was symbol-
ised for us by the Kennedys, who presented American imperialism in the liberal phrasing and middlebrow culture of
Camelot. This attracted the Canadian bourgeoisie, who liked
to believe that the society which so benefited them was also
producing human excellence. How much closer were "Jack
and Jackie" to the culture of Forest Hill and Westmount than
was the remembering rhetorician from Prince Albert. It was
natural for the *Globe and Mail* to be dazzled by the Kennedys. The villains of my book have gone down before the
crime of political assassination. Their instrument in Ottawa,
Mr. Pearson, has disappeared into whatever limbo awaits the
ambitions of self-righteousness. In the U.S. the dominant
classes now find themselves in a situation which requires a
tighter politics. They must content themselves with the
clearer, if grimmer, technocratic skill of Mr. Nixon, and even
with the direct bourgeois self-defence of Mr. Agnew
and Mr. Mitchell. We are quite proud of our "show-biz"
technocrat in Ottawa, when the U.S. can no longer afford
that luxury.

In such a situation Canadians are less impelled to rush headlong towards continental integration. On the surface there are many stirrings of nationalism. Indeed, nationalism has a clearer place, even in the present Liberal administration, than it ever had in the King, St. Laurent or Pearson eras of that party. Mr. Trudeau's policies may be inadequate, vacillating, and tailored to please the dominant powers, yet they still show traces of care about Canada which could not have been present in Howe's worship of the corporation, or in the capitalist "internationalism" of Mr. Pearson. Although Mr. Trudeau seems willing to go along with the central Liberal tradition of never offending the large corporations on substantial issues, he seems to make small concessions to our supposed independence. Most hopeful is that among the young, (sometimes in formal politics but more often outside it), the desire for independence is greater than for many generations. Unlike the generation of 1945, which scrambled into the corporations, they have a realistic suspicion of corporation capitalism, and this is after all the negative *sine qua non* of any nationalism.

Nevertheless, below the surface the movement towards integration continues. The immediate reason for this is our position in the empire. We are not in that empire as are the exploited colonies of South America, but rather with the intimacy of a younger brother status. We have all the advantages of that empire, the wealth which pours in from all over the world, the technology which comes to us through the multinational corporations. Yet, because we have formal political independence, we can keep out of some of the dirty work necessary to that empire. We make money from Vietnam; but we do not have to send our sons there. We are like the child of some stockbroker who can enjoy the fruits of his father's endeavours by living the swinging life, but likes to exclude

from his mind where the money comes from. Like most other
human beings, Canadians want it both ways. We want
through formal nationalism to escape the disadvantages of
the American dream; yet we also want the benefits of junior
membership in the empire. Unfortunately it is the dominant
classes in our society who gain particularly from that membership. This general position has been put most absurdly by
the Liberal leader in Quebec, M. Bourassa: "American technology, French culture" – as if technology were something
external (e.g. machines) and not itself a spirit which excludes
all that is alien to itself. As Heidegger has said, technique is
the metaphysic of the age.

Lying behind the immediate decisions arising from our status within the empire is the deeper question of the fate of any
particularity in the technological age. What happens to
nationalist strivings when the societies in question are given
over, at the very level of faith, to the realisation of the technological dream? At the core of that faith is service to the
process of universalization and homogenization. "The one
best means" must after all be the same in Chicago, Hamilton, and Dusseldorf. How much difference can there be
between societies whose faith in "the one best means" tran-
scends even communist and capitalist differences? The distinction will surely be minimal between two nations which
share a continent and a language, especially when the smaller
of the two has welcomed with open arms the chief instruments of its stronger brother – the corporations.

Although our present political status gives us certain
advantages over the U.S., it entails certain disadvantages. Life
as little brother often leads to political naivety and even self-
righteousness. We have not produced such a firmly defined
opposition as have the United States. Not so many of us have
been forced to look unflinchingly into the face of Moloch. In

stressing this disadvantage, I do not imply the terrible Marxist doctrine that we can encourage great political evils
because they are a necessity to later political good. The
evil of this doctrine was exposed when the communists
espoused, in its name, political polarization during the
Weimar Republic.

This book was written too much from anger and too little
from irony. The ambiguity of the English-speaking Canadian
tradition was therefore not made evident. Our hope lay in
the belief that on the northern half of this continent we could
build a community which had a stronger sense of the common good and of public order than was possible under the
individualism of the American capitalist dream. The original
sources of that hope in the English-speaking part of our society lay in certain British traditions which had been denied in
the American revolution. But the American liberalism which
we had to oppose, itself came out of the British tradition –
the liberalism of Locke and Adam Smith, – which was also
to become dominant in England as well as in the U.S., and
which reached its apotheosis and decadence there in the
thought of Keynes and Moore and Forster. The sense of the
common good standing against capitalist individualism
depended in English-speaking Canada on a tradition of
British conservatism which was itself largely beaten in Great
Britain by the time it was inherited by Canadians. Our pio-
neering conditions also made individualist capitalist greed the
overwhelming force among our elite. But such a spirit could
not but express itself as continentalist from the time of the
Annexation Manifesto to the present. Many Canadians – in
church and state and education – worked against this spirit,
and hoped to incarnate certain older traditions from western
Europe. But one of the reasons their dreams were vain was
that they tried to hold onto these things through Britishness,

just at a time when western Europe was turning away from its pre-progressive past and surrendering to the same technological Moloch of war and peace which was to reach its height in the U.S. To put the matter crudely: the irony is seen when one contemplates the fact that in our century the British have abased themselves before American capitalism for the sake of beating the Germans, only to find after two supposed victories that the Germans are more important to their masters than they are themselves. The twentieth century was not a period in which it was wise to rely on British traditions as counterattractions to the American dream. Yet these were what we had.

I emphasize this failure in irony because many simple people (particularly journalists and professors) took it to be a lament for the passing of a British dream of Canada. It was rather a lament for the romanticism of the original dream. Only a fool could have lived in Toronto in the 1920s and 1930s without recognizing that any British tradition of the common good which transcended contract was only a veneer. Today, the British tradition means that Mr. E.P. Taylor, who has given his life to integrating this country into the capitalist empire, still in the 1970s finds it impossible to pronounce the words "Kentucky Derby" in the proper American fashion.

A serious criticism of the book has been that to write in terms of inevitability (call it if you will fate) is to encourage the flaccid will which excuses the sin of despair in the name of necessity. By writing of the defeat of Canadian nationalism, one encourages in a small way the fulfilment of the prophecy. Most men, when in a weak position, need immanent hopes to keep alive their will to fight against odds. This has obviously been one of the great strengths of Marxists. Their belief that history was on their side has given them the strength to live with courage in times of difficulty and defeat.

The accusation would be that I had no business to write of the defeat of Canadian nationalism because in so doing I may have encouraged it.

To answer such a criticism would require a careful discussion of the idea of the noble delusion – that is, the doctrine that the health of any society depends on those who have practical authority being attached to virtue, and that this attachment can often only be sustained by opinions which are less than perfectly true. Whatever might be said of that doctrine, it clearly must be applied in writing with prudence – in the light of the circumstances at hand. We live in an era when most of our public men are held by ignoble delusions – generally a mixture of technological progressivism and personal self-assertion – all that is left of official liberalism in the English-speaking world. In such circumstances a writer has a greater responsibility to ridicule the widespread ignoble delusions than to protect the few remaining beliefs which might result in nobility. In an age when the alternatives often seem to be between planetary destruction and planetary tyranny (and when these alternatives are obvious products of the ignoble delusions of "the age of reason"), protecting romantic hopes of Canadian nationalism is a secondary responsibility.

This criticism is related to a more important one. My writings have often been called pessimistic. The words "optimistic" and "pessimistic" came into the tradition around the thought of Leibniz, and Voltaire's rather shallow criticism of him. They were words describing men's interpretation of the whole. I think the words should be reserved for this purpose and not used loosely about other people's feeling states or particular predictions. It would be the height of pessimism to believe that our society could go on in its present directions without bringing down upon itself catastrophes. To believe the foregoing would be pessimism, for it would imply that the nature of things does not bring forth human excellence.

Dundas, 1970.

Foreword to the Carleton Library Edition
PETER C. EMBERLEY

IN HIS 1970 INTRODUCTION to *Lament for a Nation*, Professor George Grant modestly expressed doubt whether his study had an enduring importance beyond the particular circumstances occasioning its appearance. He questioned whether his appeal to the distinctiveness of our political heritage would strike a responsive chord in a generation witnessing other historical events and participating in new social experiences. Yet, Grant's modesty aside, one should urge readers to renew their acquaintance with his passionate defense of our Canadian identity, if for no other reason than that we are still, and perhaps to an even greater extent, subject to widespread homogenizing, continentalist forces which have been shaping our destiny for the past two decades. For those whose lives have been deeply affected by massive continental economic restructuring, who have begun to experience the political and social implications of living within the new continental trade region formed under the North American Free Trade Agreement, and who are attempting to navigate between equally powerful globalizing forces and the recrudescence of fragmenting local attachments, Grant's tocsin still warns with unsurpassed clarity of the dangerous shoals surrounding us.

Grant's essay is of enduring importance, however, beyond the similarities between our own time and the historical circumstances within which *Lament for a Nation* was written.

With this study, Professor Grant opened Canadian public debate, with frankness and depth, to include the most fundamental and perennial questions a nation must ask itself about the full meaning of its own political existence. He challenged us to reflect on the unique possibilities and limits constituting our destiny as Canadians. If it took as its point of departure Diefenbaker's opposition to nuclear warheads for the Bomarc missiles and his subsequent resistance to Kennedy's continental defense initiative, Grant's study moved rapidly to broader questions concerning the difficult fate of a people in the modern age, whose experiences and ways of life evidence a complexity and depth greater than the equally pressing force of technological progress. How do forms of human existence in which people traditionally found meaning for their lives, Grant asked, stand in relation to the modern project on behalf of universal liberation and mastery of nature? Was it our fate as modern beings to live out the aridity and flatness of the culture defining the technological empire south of us? Were there phenomena in our own heritage, he challenged, which could sustain some resistance and provide moral ballast to the apparent soulless world order forming around us? Professor Grant confronted, in these questions, the complex issue of how to preserve some compass points amidst forces denying their relevance.

Lament for a Nation should be respected as a masterpiece of political meditation. A meditation raises the reader from what is familiar and near, to a level in which the recollection of experiences and understandings reveals what is most enduring in our human existence. It demands that we reflect on the tension between our particular historical existence and the greater whole of which we are a part. A meditation closes by returning its participants to the familiar and near, having disclosed how they are necessarily invested with what is highest and most enduring.

A political meditation can only be written and understood by those who enjoy friendship with the regime they inhabit. Such civic friendships are not only expressed as contentment with the peace and security afforded by the regime. As Grant admits, *Lament for a Nation* is written both in anger and in sadness. But, it is also written out of friendship. Anger is in this case the manifestation of righteous indignation, occasioned by a sense of injustice, and born from loyalty to and trust in a tradition of practices to which one believes one owes an allegiance. It draws its life from friendship to a tradition which preserves a "precious good" worthy of great sacrifices. Sadness is the appropriate response to the temporal vicissitudes all friendships must undergo, a melancholic witnessing to the changes and reassessments to which all life is subject. Grant's expressions of anger and sadness simply capture the percolations of friendship, and for this reason should not be seen as arising from resentment or loss of spirit. His is a sort of chastening rhetoric, permitted only by friends; friends whose melancholy works like a homeopathic draught of wormwood.

Lament for a Nation, like Professor Grant's other works, is grounded on the principle that our interpretation of ourselves and what we perceive as meaningful is, in great part, brought forward within a "destiny" or "fate" (a "primal" as he would call it) which precedes our individual efforts and enables us to be the sort of beings we are. He believed that a legacy of accomplishments and meaningful symbols could be a heritage for the present. The "pre-judgements" and "fore-thoughts" of the primal we inhabit provide the substance of our debates and our actions; they compose the "web" in which all our intercourse occurs. But Grant did not believe that we were ineluctably immured in this historical horizon. We could respond to our "primal," perhaps by resenting its drawing power, or by trying to master it and subject its contents to different values. Ours could also be a response of openness, a reverent respect for the distinctive political and moral possibilities inherent within it. The wager for Canadians was how we would respond to our "primal."

This response would be complex. It is our difficult destiny as Canadians in North America, Professor Grant pointed out, to be faced with contradicting "primals." First, we were part of a tradition whose founding myths, political symbols, and autochthonous experiences constitute our sense of place and belongingness to a land and its culture. Our own is not simply space and time, it is a territory and a history. It is a home crafted by tory strains of respect for the community or nation and recognition of the appropriate cultural practices needed to sustain orderly, political right; by Catholic and Anglican strains of loving stewardship to the divine and a sense of "owingness" to what is beyond human will; and by diverse British philanthropic strains of charity and equality of condition. This had to be contrasted with an empire to the south whose politics affirmed the primacy of individuals and the value of technical skills; whose religion looked, via Reformed Calvinism, to the sovereignty and creativity of the divine will in history as the paradigm for human initiative; and whose economics sanctioned virtually unhindered self-interested enterprise. Our country, Grant would say, was to be different from the United States: it would be a society which was more ordered, more reasonable, more caring, less violent, and less enthused by reckless dreams.

Existing in tension with this heritage, however, was another destiny, equally composing our way in the world. What we are, Grant explained, is also constituted by a milieu whose logic and direction had been unfolding since the beginning of modernity, with the American empire as its most expressive manifestation: being as technology. Grant, indebted here to Heidegger, was later to call the technological spirit of modernity a "complete ontological package," meaning that our institutions, our programs, our laws, our behaviours, our amusements and our self-understandings were all fundamentally echoing its logic. A philosophy of reason as domination over nature, a politics of imperial, bureaucratic administration, a public discourse of efficiency, and a sociology of adjustment and equilibrium were forging, as so many specialized arts of modern technology, a new way for us. Grant's shorthand version of how technology was reshaping us was to speak of its "universalizing" and "homogenizing" effect. Contained within these terms were complex reflections on the modern dream of universal liberation and the prospect of universal tyranny, and on the moral hopes associated with equality and the reality of creeping sameness. Taken together, he was to demonstrate, technology involved a fundamental reshaping of the human spirit and the gradual eclipse or transformation of human experiences that in the past had provided us with moral and intellectual ballast. An assessment of this second destiny was not as easy as one might expect. It would be otiose, Grant never tired of reminding, to overlook the moral promise and concrete achievements of modern technology. It had made possible, in a way never believed possible, the actualization of the duty of charity and the extension of individual freedom. While it did not carry forth the full spirituality of Christianity's vision of a universal free and equal community, the regime of modern technology had erased the oppressive hierarchies and insular parochialisms impeding the actualization of that vision. While no one should deny this was progress, the question remained, At what cost?

As Grant argues here, and more thematically in his later books, technological progress could not be separated from an accompanying transformation of the human spirit; a transformation which made it impossible to unite the new social controls with traditional moralities and politics. Universalizing and homogenizing, technology's driving principle of "efficiency" demanded the suppression of local differences, particular loyalties, and credible resistances. Whatever lingering pockets of "autochthony" might declare opposition, the spirit of the regime – sustained by its continental ruling class of technicians and administrators, and the officially sanctioned discourse of instrumentality and efficiency – regarded their opposition as nothing more than folly or sentimentality. The new regime, whatever value the fruits of its technical arts and sciences, was a universal tyranny, disagreeably out of tune with the principle that had once sustained the Western world and particularly its North American experiment, namely cultural pluralism and freedom of the spirit.

The fate of Canada was a microcosm of the confrontation of all peoples with.the powerfully transforming forces of the West. The expectation that Canadians might recall what within their "primal" constituted a "precious good" worth preserving, or what might be testimony to a spiritually more profound way of being human, had been annulled in the realization that any distinctiveness in Canada's way of life, its skills, and practices, could only appear now as stylized, abstract images circulating through the homogenizing processes of technological efficiency. The same would be true around the globe. The conservative and communitarian strands in our heritage, once understood as containing enduring concepts of what is good for humanity, could now only be seen as mere political ideology or a set of values.

Against this, no simple appeal to the spirit or rootedness of our past sense of belonging to the land could be relevant. To think of containing and embalming the distinctive virtues of that time would be to condemn oneself to antiquarianism or romanticism, if not worse. There could be no return to a past, nor should the spirit of modernity be dampened by willing away what had come to be. Grant, following Nietzsche, had continuously warned of the poisonous "resentment" that lay at the heart of wishing away time's "it was" – a poison that could deprive life of vitality and confidence.

Lament for a Nation is, however, more than a lament of a passing good and a dissection of the non-viability of nationalist or conservative discourse. If it demonstrates the public irrelevance of those discourses, it does not assume their theoretical emptiness. Indeed, the meditation has the effect, with its powerful symbols and chastening rhetoric, to evoke a bittersweet remembrance of our foundations, of the expectations we have of our heroes, and of different stories we tell of our battles and accords. Such remembrance, at the very least, tugs at vestiges of the primal which continues to inspire our self-interpretation. How else could the passionate appeals of Western, Québec, and Maritime nationalists evoke such enthusiasm; how else could our continuing efforts to negotiate and renegotiate satisfactory economic and military ties to our continental neighbours give rise to such debate and emotion; why else would regional separatist agitation inspire such a groundswell of support to renew our political institutions?

The questions Professor Grant demanded we confront still lie at the centre of our current political debates. How can Canada preserve fragments of a way of life and of understandings whose public relevance is doubtful to our ruling elites? Is it necessary to capitulate to the agenda of continentalist expansion, and what are the costs of such multinational efficiency to the Canadian workforce, its culture, social programs, and political independence? Is the promise of a global village, liberated to the latest technological contrivances, the reality of a universal tyranny? And beyond this, have the forces of progress unleashed further forces which are extinguishing not only the confidence in progress but also the commitment to the purposes we believe to be furthered by that progress? Finally, can a regime which has eclipsed the public relevance of experiences of either tradition or transcendence, be humanly satisfying?

Grant posed questions in *Lament for a Nation* which are at the heart of Canada's existence as a nation. He himself offered no simple answers but illuminated the inevitable complexity and ambiguity of such questions as the proper intellectual territory of inquiry for the thinking mind. He was optimistic. We have been able to safeguard the complexity and ambiguity of those answers, and hence our humanity, by moral and political practices which respect plurality, dignity, and our higher purposes, and which abjure quick solutions, absolute certainties, and radical transformations. Grant asked us to ensure the same type of moderation for the present and the future.

A chastening rhetoric both cleanses and purifies. If we were to speak of the enduring significance of *Lament for a Nation*, it would be that Professor Grant challenges us to respond to the deepest demands of our modern existence, both as dwellers on a continent defined by a great imperial power and as participants in the complex project of modernity. He tries to teach us, against all odds, how we can still see what is beautiful and good in our own. Grant asks us to be aware of traces of practices, understandings, ways of life, and lived-experience which are pre-technological in our cultural and political legacy and manifest in "the evident experience of living." He knew we had also to accept the difficult tensions of technological society. His advice is a prescription of steering between local parochialism on the one hand and the deracinated life of the modern universal and homogeneous state on the other. It is a prescription demanding attentiveness and courage.

In the wake of the consensuses and discords of the Meech Lake Agreement and the Charlottetown Accord, the recurring threat of regional separatism, not to say fragmentation along innumerable social cleavages; the controversies and opportunities opened by the new continental trade partnership; and the fractious state of affairs at the international level where Canada continually reassesses its proper role, the courage and moderation counselled by Professor Grant seem as appropriate today as they were in 1963. It is just as important to remind today's political leaders how vital it is to place these new departures in the most comprehensive context – historical and philosophical. This is especially important if we are one day to be called before the bar of history to justify and explain our watershed decisions. Our age seems forever animated by a sort of new-world visionary politics on which such policies seem to ride forward, and by awesome technological power at our behest which can quell all resistances. This makes ours the time requiring the most sustained, responsible, and profound public debates concerning our continued existence. For such debates, *Lament for a Nation* has identified a set of symbols and a cosmion of meaning which might guide us with common sense and integrity, still understandable as the great guarantors of public decency.

Carleton University
1994

Lament for a Nation

Chapter One

NEVER HAS SUCH A TORRENT of abuse been poured on any Canadian figure as that during the years from 1960 to 1965. Never have the wealthy and the clever been so united as they were in their joint attack on Mr. John Diefenbaker. It has made life pleasant for the literate classes to know that they were on the winning side. Emancipated journalists were encouraged to express their dislike of the small-town Protestant politician, and they knew they would be well paid by the powerful for their efforts. Suburban matrons and professors knew that there was an open season on Diefenbaker, and that jokes against him at cocktail parties would guarantee the medal of sophistication. New agreements were produced. Such a progressive intellectual as F.H. Underhill ridiculed Diefenbaker in the same accents as the editorials of the *Globe and Mail*. Socialist members of parliament united with the representatives of Toronto and Montreal business to vote his government from office. In my parish in southern Ontario, on the Sunday before the election of 1963, the Holy Eucharist was offered for "stable government," well expressing the unanimity of bourgeois intention. Only the rural and small-town people voted for Diefenbaker *en masse*, but such people are members of neither the ruling nor the opinion-forming classes.

The tide of abuse abated after the election of 1963. The establishment thought that it had broken Diefenbaker and could now afford to patronize him. But Diefenbaker has refused to play dead. He has shown himself capable of something the wealthy and the clever rarely understand – the virtue of courage. The patronizing airs are turning once more into abuse; the editorials and the "news" become increasingly vindictive.

It is interesting to speculate why Diefenbaker raised the concentrated wrath of the established classes. Most of his critics claim that he is dominated by ambition, almost to the point of egomania. They also claimed (while he was still in office) that he was dangerous because he was an astute politician who put personal power first. Yet his actions turned the ruling class into a pack howling for his blood. Astute politicians, who are only interested in political power, simply do not act this way. There must be something false or something missing in this description of his actions. To search for a consistent description is partly why I have written this book.

The search must be related to the title of this meditation. To lament is to cry out at the death or at the dying of something loved. This lament mourns the end of Canada as a sovereign state. Political laments are not usual in the age of progress, because most people think that society always moves forward to better things. Lamentation is not an indulgence in despair or cynicism. In a lament for a child's death, there is not only pain and regret, but also celebration of passed good.

I cannot but remember such things were
That were most precious to me.

In Mozart's great threnody, the Countess sings of *la memoria di quel bene*. One cannot argue the meaninglessness of the world from the facts of evil, because what could evil deprive us of, if we had not some prior knowledge of good? The situation of absolute despair does not allow a man to write. In the theatre of the absurd, dramatists like Ionesco and Beckett do not escape this dilemma. They pretend to absolute despair and yet pour out novels and plays. When a man truly despairs, he does not write; he commits suicide. At the other extreme, there are the saints who know that the destruction of good serves the supernatural end; therefore they cannot lament. Those who write laments may have heard the propositions of the saints, but they do not know that they are true. A lament arises from a condition that is common to the majority of men, for we are situated between despair and absolute certainty.

I have implied that the existence of a sovereign Canada served the good. But can the disappearance of an unimportant nation be worthy of serious grief? For some older Canadians it can. Our country is the only political entity to which we have been trained to pay allegiance. Growing up in Ontario, the generation of the 1920s took it for granted that they belonged to a nation. The character of the country was self-evident. To say it was British was not to deny it was North American. To be a Canadian was to be a unique species of North American. Such alternatives as F.H. Underhill's – "Stop being British if you want to be a nationalist" – seemed obviously ridiculous. We were grounded in the wisdom of Sir John A. Macdonald, who saw plainly more than a hundred years ago that the only threat to nationalism was from the South, not from across the sea. To be a Canadian was to build, along with the French, a more ordered and stable society than the liberal experiment in the United States. Now that this hope has been extinguished, we are too old to be retrained by a new master. We find ourselves like fish left on the shores of a drying lake. The element necessary to our existence has passed away. As some form of political loyalty is part of the good life, and as we are not flexible enough to kneel to the rising sun, we must be allowed to lament the passing of what had claimed our allegiance. Even on a continent too dynamic to have memory, it may still be salutary to celebrate memory. The history of the race is strewn with gasping political fish. What makes the gasping comic, in the present case, is its involvement with such ambiguous and contrasting figures as Pearson and Diefenbaker.

Lamenting for Canada is inevitably associated with the tragedy of Diefenbaker. His inability to govern is linked with the inability of this country to be sovereign. In the last years, many writers have described the confusions, contradictions, and failures of the Diefenbaker government. Even when Peter Newman has exuded malice, or Blair Fraser has hidden Liberal propaganda behind the mask of impartiality, their descriptions have often been accurate. Yet their accuracy is made suspect by their total argument. They rejoice that we have back in office the party of the ruling class. They generously allow that the Liberal party had become arrogant by 1957, and that in a "democratic" system it is good to have alternative administrations. (For example, it gives our natural rulers a proper chastening.) But they never grant that, for twenty years before its defeat in 1957, the Liberal party had been pursuing policies that led inexorably to the disappearance of Canada. Its policies led to the impossibility of an alternative to the American republic being built on the northern half of this continent. They never grant that the seeds of Canada's surrender lay in Mackenzie King's régime. This fact and Diefenbaker's inchoate knowledge of it are ignored by the journalists of the establishment. They never allow that when the Conservatives came to office they were faced with a situation that would lead, if not corrected, to the disappearance of their country's independence. No credit is given to the desperate attempts of Diefenbaker and his colleagues to find alternative policies, both national and international, to those of their predecessors.

Diefenbaker's confusions and inconsistencies are, then, to be seen as essential to the Canadian fate. His administration was not an aberration from which Canada will recover under the sensible rule of the established classes. It was a bewildered attempt to find policies that were adequate to its noble cause.

The 1957 election was the Canadian people's last gasp of nationalism. Diefenbaker's government was the strident swan-song of that hope. Although the Canadian nationalist may be saddened by the failures of Diefenbaker, he is sickened by the shouts of sophisticated derision at his defeat. Those who crowed at Diefenbaker's fall did not understand the policies of government that were essential if Canada was to survive. In their derision they showed, whether they were aware of it or not, that they really paid allegiance to the homogenized culture of the American Empire.

This meditation is limited to lamenting. It makes no practical proposals for our survival as a nation. It argues that Canada's disappearance was a matter of necessity. But how can one lament necessity – or, if you will, fate? The noblest of men love it; the ordinary accept it; the narcissists rail against it. But I lament it as a celebration of memory; in this case, the memory of that tenuous hope that was the principle of my ancestors. The insignificance of that hope in the endless ebb and flow of nature does not prevent us from mourning. At least we can say with Richard Hooker: "Posterity may know we have not loosely through silence permitted things to pass away as in a dream."

Chapter Two

HOW DID DIEFENBAKER CONCEIVE CANADA? Why did the men who run the country come to dislike and then fear his conception? The answers demonstrate much about Canada and its collapse.

Most journalists account for Diefenbaker's failure by the foibles of his personality. Influenced by *Time* magazine, politics is served up as gossip, and the more titillating the better. The jaded public wants to be amused; journalists have to eat well. Reducing issues to personalities is useful to the ruling class. The "news" now functions to legitimize power, not to convey information. The politics of personalities helps the legitimizers to divert attention from issues that might upset the status quo. Huntley and Brinkley are basic to the American way of life. Canadian journalists worked this way in the election of 1963. Their purposes were better served by writing of Diefenbaker's "indecision," of Diefenbaker's "arrogance," of Diefenbaker's "ambition," than by writing about American-Canadian relations. Indeed, his personality was good copy. The tragedy of his leap to unquestioned power, the messianic stance applied to administrative detail, the prairie rhetoric murdering the television – these are an essential part of the Diefenbaker years. But behind all the stories of arrogance and indecision, there are conflicts – conflicts over principles. The man had a conception of Canada that threatened the dominant classes. This encounter is the central clue to the Diefenbaker administration. The political actions of men are ultimately more serious than the gossip of *Time* and *Newsweek* will allow.

All ruling classes are produced by the societies they are required to rule. In the 1960s, state capitalism organizes a technological North America. The ruling classes are those that control the private governments (that is, the corporations) and those that control the public government which co-ordinates the activities of these corporations. North America is the base of the world's most powerful empire to date, and this empire is in competition with other empires. The civilians and soldiers who run its military operations increasingly crowd its corridors of power.[1]

Since 1960, Canada has developed into a northern extension of the continental economy. This was involved in the decisions made by C.D. Howe and his men. Our traditional role – as an exporter of raw materials (particularly to Europe) with highly protected industry in central Canada – gradually lost its importance in relation to our role as a branch-plant of American capitalism. Our ruling class is composed of the same groups as that of the United States, with the signal difference that the Canadian ruling class looks across the border for its final authority in both politics and culture. As Canada is only gradually being called upon to play a full role in United States' world policies, our military is less influential at home than is the case in the United States. Of all the aspects of our society, the military is the most directly an errand boy for the Americans.

[1] The use of the concept "American Empire" is often objected to, particularly by those who like to believe that the age of empires is over. They associate an empire with earlier patterns – the British, the Spanish, and the French – when Europeans maintained rule in distant parts of the globe by superior arms and control of the sea. But an empire does not have to wield direct political control over colonial countries. Poland and Czechoslovakia are as much part of the Russian Empire as India was of the British, or Canada and Brazil of the American. An empire is the control of one state by another. In this sense, the United States of America has an empire.

Our rulers, particularly whose who enjoy wielding power, move in and our of the corporations, the civil service, and politics. For example, Mitchell Sharp was a leading civil servant under C.D. Howe, directing the development of our resources by continental capitalism. With the fall of the Liberals, he had to move to Brazilian Traction. He had the gumption, however, to be interested in the revival of the Liberal party at its lowest ebb, and so today he exercises power as Minister of Trade and Commerce. The political members of the ruling class live more precariously than the businessmen and the civil servants, but if successful they have the pleasures of public power. For instance, it did not appear likely, before the election of 1957, that Pearson would be the leader of the Liberal party. A civil servant who had turned Minister of External Affairs was not close to the heart of those creating the new Canada from 1945 to 1957. Yet after the election of 1957, when many Liberal leaders immediately retreated into the cover of the corporations, he had the courage to stay with the inconveniences of politics. Today he and his friends have direct control over the government. On the other hand, Robert Winters, who could not stomach the inconveniences of opposition, must content himself with running Rio Tinto and York University.

From 1940 to 1957, the ruling class of this country was radically reshaped. In 1939, the United Kingdom still seemed a powerful force, and the men who ruled Canada were a part of the old Atlantic triangle. They turned almost as much to Great Britain as to the United States, economically, culturally, and politically. After 1940, the ruling class found its centre of gravity in the United States. During the long years of Liberal rule, the strength of the Conservative party was maintained by those who were still to some extent oriented toward Great Britain. The new rulers of the

conservative

Howe era inevitably backed the Liberal party; economic and political power were mutually dependent.

The old Conservative élite kept Diefenbaker from a central place in his party for many years. They ensured that the control of the party remained in Toronto. After Bennett's defeat in 1935, the Conservative party became a rump, with nearly all its strength in Ontario.[2] Diefenbaker only came to leadership because of support from the fringe areas of the country, and because the Toronto group was at the end of its tether after the failure to build a national party under Drew. When, in 1957, Diefenbaker did squeeze in, he did so in spite of the dominant classes of the Howe era. Indeed, even after the business community had thrown over Bennett for King, it continued its contributions to the Conservative party, because it is wise for the wealthy to have their feet in both the opposition and the government. Despite these contributions, large-scale business did not expect or support the defeat of the Liberal party in 1957.

The cause of that defeat was a protest by Canadians not against the principles but against the pin-pricks of the Howe régime. The new engineers were not very agile in the legitimizing of power. In 1956, the Pipe-Line Debate was a signal example of failure to legitimize power. The Liberals openly announced that our resources were at the disposal of continental capitalism. The use of closure expressed the Howe administration's contempt for the "talking shop." So much did

2 This may seem to be contradicted by the leadership in those years being in the hands of Manion and Bracken. In both cases these men were the choices of the Toronto group. For example, Bracken was supported for the leadership against Murdo Macpherson because, in 1943, the CCF was a real threat in Ontario. It was hoped that by making a farmer head of the party, the rural ridings of Ontario would remain loyal provincially. Only with Drew did the Toronto group actually have one of its own.

they identify their branch-plant society with the Kingdom of Heaven that they did not pay sufficient attention to the farmers or the outlying regions. Such regions existed for them as colonies of Montreal and Toronto. The Conservative victory was accomplished by local businessmen who felt excluded from their own country by corporation capitalism. Young men, ambitious for a life in politics, could not turn to the Liberal party, where the positions of power were well secured by the old pros. The Liberal's policy of satellite status to the United States, and their open attack on the British at the time of Suez, annoyed the residualloyalties of older Canadians.

Diefenbaker made the most of these pin-pricks in his campaign of 1957. The victory of 1958 followed as the night the day. The masses wanted a change. The business community naturally backed the successful. What did it have to fear when as orthodox a servant of business as Donald Fleming was given the finance portfolio in 1957? Quebec found it necessary to get on the bandwagon. Even Diefenbaker's nationalist rhetoric stirred the old memories. He was mistaken, however, when he imagined that such rhetoric was central to his victory. Later he was to rely on it, when it no longer brought the same response.

Within five years of gaining the largest majority in our history, Diefenbaker's government was defeated, and a new copy of the old régime was back in power. In this sense, at least, his administration had been a failure. Clearly he had not failed in sincerity, although the journalists of legitimacy even discounted that quality in him. They maintained that his nationalism was a cloak concealing the real man of ambition. But is it feasible to doubt his integrity at this point? In the Defence Crisis of 1963, his nationalism occasioned the strongest stand against satellite status that any Canadian government ever attempted. He maintained his stand even when the full power of the Canadian ruling class, the American government, and the military were brought against him. It is fair to maintain that such nationalism was misguided, but it is hardly honest to judge it to be insincere. What should be asked is: What kind of nationalism brought down on top of him the full wrath of a continental ruling class, and at the same time failed to produce feasible policies of government?

Diefenbaker saw his destiny as revivifying the Canadian nation. But what did he think that nation was? Certainly he had a profound – if romantic – sense of historical continuity. But a nation does not remain a nation only because it has roots in the past. Memory is never enough to guarantee that a nation can articulate itself in the present.[3] There must be a thrust of intention into the future. When the nation is the intimate neighbour of a dynamic empire, this necessity is even more obvious. Diefenbaker certainly saw his government as a spearhead of Canada's intention. His destiny was to revive a nation that had been disintegrating under the previous Liberal régime. Yet, because he was never specific about what Canada should be, he failed. In studying his government, one becomes aware of a series of mutually conflicting conceptions.

Diefenbaker was committed to a Canadian populism. He believed that he represented all the people and all the regions of the country. As a criminal lawyer he had learnt that the interests of the small need defending against the powerful. After 1958, he often repeated: "Everyone is against me but the people." One of his chosen models was Franklin Delano Roosevelt, and he interpreted Roosevelt's success as an appeal to the people over the heads of the great.

3 National articulation is a process through which human beings form and re-form themselves into a society to act historically. This process coheres around the intention realized in the action. See Eric Voegelin, *The New Science of Politics* (Chicago: University of Chicago Press, 1952), 37 *et seq.*

In the past, Diefenbaker's party had relied on support from the established classes in Ontario – from men whose philosophy was hardly that of the fair share. Diefenbaker contradicted his populism at the very beginning of his régime by appointing Donald Fleming the Minister of Finance. As an Ontario Tory, Fleming shared nationalism with Diefenbaker, but not populism. One of the comedies of this period was the tension between a Prime Minister set on populism and a Finance Minister who was even less Keynesian than Howe. It was ironic that Diefenbaker should have consented to a conversion loan that was obviously in the interest of the bond houses, while Fleming should have listened to his Prime Minister attacking the chartered banks over television. The tension between Diefenbaker and the business Conservatives was reconciled in the election of 1963. Nearly all the economic power deserted the Conservative party. He did not convince them with his nationalist appeals. The history of the breed does not make this surprising. The wealthy rarely maintain their nationalism when it is in conflict with the economic drive of the day.

By 1957, many Canadians could do with a spot of populism. The Howe-Abbott-Harris régime had run the country in the interests of Toronto-Montreal and their representatives in other provinces. The régime was building an expansionist society for the entrepreneur, the salesman, and the stock-broker. Diefenbaker's increased welfare payments and aid to "outlying regions" showed him turning to the people. But populist democracy is a dying force in contemporary America. It belonged to the Saskatchewan or Wisconsin of Diefenbaker's youth, not to those who work for Simpson's-Sears or General Motors. When he combined his prairie populism with the private-enterprise ideology of the small town, it made a strange mixture. Diefenbaker, the foe of bureaucracy and planning, went ill with Diefenbaker, the admirer of Roosevelt. Nor did

his talk of free enterprise belong to an older Canadian conservatism, which had used public power to achieve national purposes. The Conservative party had, after all, created Ontario
Hydro, the CNR, the Bank of Canada, and the CBC.

Populism plus small-town free enterprise was entirely inadequate, and it could not come to terms with the society that
had arisen since the war. Central Canada had grown into an
industrialized complex. Any government to remain in office
had to meet the new needs of this sector. A government set
upon-national revival had to do even more: it had to reverse
the trend that was taking the keystone of the country and integrating it with Michigan and New York. Diefenbaker's administration did neither. He did not meet the needs of this
heartland, and he realized no nationalist ends. His remarkable
achievement was to alienate the support of both the rulers and
the ruled in both Ontario and Quebec.

The Conservatives came to power at a time when world economics were less favourably disposed to Canada than at any
time since the war. The less prosperous felt the pinches of the
recession which started in 1957. Diefenbaker did not meet this
situation with any co-ordinated economic plan. The government only alleviated the growing unemployment by winter
works, and scarcely touched upon the problems caused by
automation. Diefenbaker lost the wide support he had once
held among the ordinary people of Ontario. Those who were
suffering came to think his nationalism was the usual political
yapping. Once more the Conservative party was associated
with unemployment and recession.

At the same time, Diefenbaker succeeded in antagonizing
the citadels of corporate power. His talk of free enterprise
meant no more to corporate wealth than Barry Goldwater's
did in 1964. During the Howe era, the wealthy had become
used to running the country; they assumed it was natural there
should be an identity of interests between themselves and the

Liberal government. It is quite clear that this identity was far less complete under the Conservatives, despite Donald Fleming, than under the Liberals. The Conservatives handled the machine of state capitalism less skilfully than had the Liberal smoothies.

Not only did Diefenbaker lose political support in industrial Canada; he did not accomplish the work of economic nationalism. The "northern vision" was a pleasant extra, but no substitute for national survival. During his years in office, American control grew at a quickening rate. This was the crucial issue in 1957. If Canada was to survive, the cornerstone of its existence was the Great Lakes region. The population in that area was rushing toward cultural and economic integration with the United States. Any hope for a Canadian nation demanded some reversal of the process, and this could only be achieved through concentrated use of Ottawa's planning and control. After 1940, nationalism had to go hand in hand with some measure of socialism. Only nationalism could provide the political incentive for planning; only planning could restrain the victory of continentalism

Later I will argue that no such combination was possible, and therefore our nation was bound to disappear. To write of "ifs" in history is always foolish. Nevertheless, if Diefenbaker had been a realistic nationalist, he would have had to try some such policy. He would have had to appeal over the heads of corporation capitalism to the masses of Ontario and Quebec. He would have had to mobilize the electorate to support the use of Ottawa's power for nationalist purposes. Above all, he would have had to have known that the corporation élite was basically anti-national.

Perhaps a criminal lawyer who had spent his life between Prince Albert and Ottawa could remain unaware of what had happened in central Canada since 1940. After his sweeping victory of 1958, Diefenbaker even seems to have thought that he had become a leader of "all the people," a conception that corporation capitalism could never take seriously. Had he forgotten why he had been kept by the traditional Ontario classes from the leadership of his party for so long, and how he had come into power in 1957? Never in Canadian history had a party come to power with fewer debts to large business than in the election of 1957. But Diefenbaker seems to have been blinded into believing that the powerful of central Canada could still be appealed to as "my fellow Canadians," and were not committed to continentalism by the very nature of what they did. He seems to have been blinded into believing that "Canadianism" could provide the basis for a harmony of interests between his populist nationalism and the new central Canada. The Canada he thought about was not the country he was required to govern. There is something naive about Diefenbaker's attacks on Toronto and Montreal business in the 1963 election, particularly in the light of the economic policies his government had pursued from 1958 to 1962. It is not surprising that the only literate and established voice on the side of Diefenbaker in the election of 1963 was Senator Grattan O'Leary, who was himself caught in the trap of romantic nationalism. Senator O'Leary also was a supporter of both nationalism and capitalism. He could presumably combine the two because he thought the leaders of Canadian capitalism after 1940 were still nationalists. There seems less excuse for such nonsense from the publisher of a great eastern newspaper than from a western lawyer. It is, nevertheless, startling that the western lawyer could still believe capitalists were nationalists after a term as Prime Minister. In short, Diefenbaker did not understand the economic implications of Canadian nationalism; he could not appraise the class structure realistically, and therefore he could not formulate the economic policies that were necessary if nationalism was to be more than rhetoric and romance. Even after his defeat, he does not seem to have learnt these lessons. As Leader of the Opposition, he attacked the measures put forward by Walter Gordon to limit the control of this country by American capital.

Diefenbaker's confusion of populism, free enterprise, and nationalism can be seen in his dealings with James Coyne, the Governor of the Bank of Canada. Leaving aside the legal rights of the Bank or the behaviour of the Governor or the Government, it is clear that Coyne was a firm Canadian.[4] He advocated a "tight-money" nationalism that would protect Canada from foreign control. This may not have been the most effective protection, but it was at least one viable alternative. Diefenbaker rejected it. He also rejected the only other possible nationalist alternative – stringent governmental control of investment.

The free-enterprise assumptions of the Diefenbaker administration led to actions that were obviously anti-national. In appointing the Glassco Commission as an equivalent to the Hoover Commission, the government seemed to be appealing to an element of the American "conservative" tradition. The civil service was investigated by the head of Brazilian Traction. Although such "conservatism" may be appropriate to the United States, it cannot be to Canada, where limiting the civil service in the name of free enterprise simply strengthens the power of the private governments. Such strengthening must be anti-nationalist because the corporations are continental.

Diefenbaker's relations with the civil service invite the writing of a picaresque novel. By including these strained relations under his failures, I do not imply that the fault lay all on his side. Too many civil servants had too closely identified them-

4 One complication was that Coyne came from an old Liberal family. The affair illustrated Diefenbaker's failure to forget old differences when great issues were at stake.

selves with Liberal men and Liberal measures before 1957,
and some of these did not show the proper loyalty to the
elected government after 1957. Some of the senior civil servants were certain they knew what was best for Canada, both
internally and externally, and they were not willing to accept
the fact that elected leaders could sensibly advocate alternative
policies. In the summer of 1963, the photograph of Pearson
being welcomed back to office by the deputy ministers showed
how far the British conception of the civil service had disappeared.[5] Nevertheless, that Diefenbaker failed to win the
respect of the civil service was a disaster. No modern state can
be run without great authority in the hands of its non-elected
officials. In such an uncertain nation as Canada, the civil service is perhaps the essential instrument by which nationhood
is preserved. The power of Ottawa has to be skilfully used by
politicians to balance the enormous anti-national forces concentrated in the economic capitals of Toronto and Montreal. If
Diefenbaker was to foster nationalism, he needed to win the
respect of the civil service. The best civil servants were devoted
to both the British account of their function and the conception of a sovereign Canadian nation. Only under Alvin Hamilton was a team of civil servants brought in to realize new
goals.

It was from George Drew that Diefenbaker inherited the
free-enterprise policy of limiting the crown corporations. The
Conservatives had long supported the Canadian Pacific Air-
lines in Parliament. It soon became evident that their objections
to the Pipeline had been only constitutional. They did not
object to the control of public resources by private and foreign

5 The question will be raised later whether the civil service could have
been persuaded to co-operate with nationalist policies, or whether
its leading personnel were too deeply involved with international
administration.

capitalists, but simply to the way Howe had pushed that control through Parliament. The administration's policy toward broadcasting is extraordinarily difficult to reconcile with any consistent nationalism. The Conservatives had long advocated a reassessment of broadcasting policy and the creation of a supervisory power to stand above both the CBC and the private broadcasters. For years Fleming had been advocating more power for private broadcasters, and he had gained support for his party when they really needed it. The Conservatives also justifiably felt that the CBC, then as today, gave too great prominence to the Liberal view of Canada. The broadcasting policy of the Conservatives was a compromise between various elements in the party. Diefenbaker and Nowlan restrained the Toronto Tories from an all-out attack on the CBC. But the Board of Broadcast Governors was implemented; a private television network was established; licences for television stations were ladled out to prosperous party supporters. Thus the Conservative party became identified with an attack on one of the central national institutions. It was forgotten that the CBC had been established by a Conservative government under Bennett, in order to maintain national control over broadcasting and to prevent the airwaves being used simply for private gain. The encouragement of private broadcasting must be anti-nationalist: the purpose of private broadcasting is to make money, and the easiest way to do this is to import canned American programs appealing to the lowest common denominator of the audience. Diefenbaker's policy was not even politically successful. John Bassett did not have the stuff of loyalty, and turned on Diefenbaker in 1963.

The most bewildering aspect of Diefenbaker's nationalism was his failure to find effective French-Canadian colleagues. The keystone of a Canadian nation is the French fact; the slightest knowledge of history makes this platitudinous. English-speaking Canadians who desire the survival of their nation have to co-operate with those who seek the continuance of Franco-American civilization. The failure of Diefenbaker to act on this maxim was his most tragic mistake. The election tactic of 1957, by which the Conservatives made no appeal to French Canada, helped to gain them an initial plurality. This may have been necessary after all the years of Liberal doubletalk. The cynical belief that Quebec would go along with the winning side proved correct in 1958. How, on so base a motive, did Diefenbaker expect to build a permanent loyalty to the Conservative cause among a sophisticated and threatened people? With fifty Quebec seats behind him from 1958 to 1962, Diefenbaker does not seem to have sought serious French lieutenants who could mediate the interests of their people to the rest of the country. He seems to have contented himself with the rag and bobtail of the *Union Nationale*. Despite present propaganda, there were noble elements in that party. Even after the death of Duplessis, in September of 1959, Diefenbaker does not seem to have tried to bring such obvious Quebec conservatives as Bertrand into his cabinet. Duplessis's death was followed immediately by that of his successor, J.M.P. Sauvé, in January of 1960. This was the deepest blow that Canadian conservatism ever sustained. Sauvé could have become the first French-Canadian Conservative Prime Minister. However, this disaster need not have prevented Diefenbaker from seeking out other leaders from the *Union Nationale*.

There was one aspect of Diefenbaker's nationalism that was repugnant to thoughtful French Canadians, however attractive to English-speaking Liberals and New Canadians. He appealed to one united Canada, in which individuals would have equal rights irrespective of race and religion; there would be no first- and second-class citizens. As far as the civil rights of individuals are concerned, this is obviously an acceptable doctrine. Nevertheless, the rights of the individual do not encompass the rights of nations, liberal doctrine to the contrary. The French Canadians had entered Confederation not to protect the rights of the individual but the rights of a nation. They did not want to be swallowed up by that sea which Henri Bourassa had called *"l'américanisme saxonisant."* Diefenbaker's prairie experience had taught him to understand the rights of ethnic and religious communities, such as the Ukrainians and the Jews. He was no petty Anglo-Saxon homogenizer who wanted everybody to be the same. He had defended the rights of communities to protect their ancient cultural patterns. But in what way was this different from the United States, where Polish and Greek Americans keep their remembrances while accepting the general ends of the Republic? The French-Canadian nation, with its unique homeland and civilization, is quite a different case. The appeal of a nation within a nation is more substantial than that of the Ukrainians or the Jews. For Diefenbaker, the unity of all Canadians is a final fact. His interpretation of federalism is basically American. It could not encompass those who were concerned with being a nation, only those who wanted to preserve charming residual customs.

This failure to recognize the rights of French Canadians, *qua* community, was inconsistent with the roots of Canadian nationalism. One distinction between Canada and the United States has been the belief that Canada was predicated on the rights of nations as well as on the rights of individuals. American nationalism was, after all, founded on the civil rights of individuals in just as firm a way as the British appeal to liberty was founded on these rights. As the price of that liberty, American society has always demanded that all autonomous communities be swallowed up into the common culture. This was demanded during the Civil War; it was demanded of each immigrant; it is still the basis of the American school system. Diefenbaker appealed to a principle that was more American than Canadian. On this principle, the French Canadians might as well be asked to be homogenized straight into the American Republic. In so far as he did not distinguish between the rights of individuals and the rights of nations, Diefenbaker showed himself to be a liberal rather than a conservative.

To explain the failure of prairie nationalism to understand French Canada, I must turn to the older quarrels that have beset the nation. The two original peoples, French and Catholic, British and Protestant, united precariously in their desire not to be part of the great Republic; but their reasons were quite different. This union was precarious partly because the preponderant classes of British stock were determined that the Canadian nation should support the international policies of the British Empire, whereas the French were either indifferent or hostile to these policies. In the Boer War and the World Wars of 1914 and 1939, the English-speaking Canadians forced their determination on the French. Many of the Conservatives who came to power with Diefenbaker – Gordon Churchill, Alvin Hamilton, Douglas Harkness, George Pearkes, George Hees – were men of the 1939 war. They had taken many of their views of French Canada from their bitterness over the Conscription Crisis, in which Mackenzie King had seemed to support French isolationism. Diefenbaker and Howard Green were of the generation that had seen Canadian nationalism and pro-Britishness closely united. It was this that gave their nationalism some real bite in an era swamped by continentalism. It is well to remember that the anti-British nationalists of English-speaking Canada in the 1930s have nearly all shown the emptiness of their early protestations by becoming consistent continentalists later on. Nevertheless, the very tradition that bred so intense a nationalism in Diefenbaker and Green and Churchill inhibited them from coming to terms with French Canada and finding a base for the Conservative party in Quebec. In the Defence Election of 1963, it was

a sad fact for Canadian nationalism that Green and Diefenbaker were unable to find any support for their policies in
Quebec, although they were a government keeping nuclear
arms off Canadian soil. By this stage in our history, Diefenbaker's and Green's nationalism was taking the form of a new
kind of neutralism, a simple refusal to accept any demand
from the present imperialism. It might have been thought that
such a policy would have appealed to elements in Quebec.
Indeed, to maintain such a policy Diefenbaker needed that
support. It was not forthcoming. It was impossible for prairie
nationalists and French-Canadian nationalists to get together.
During the five years of his immense power, Diefenbaker had
not encouraged French-Canadians to feel sympathy for the
nationalism he advocated, and populism in Quebec had turned
to the Social Credit movement. The very nature of Diefenbaker's Protestantism made him unsympathetic to Catholic
Quebec. He even broke with tradition and did not appoint an
Ontario Catholic to his Cabinet – this during a period when
the Catholic population was a stronger force than ever before.
Only after dissolution in 1963 did he appoint Frank McGee to
his Cabinet.

Diefenbaker's nationalism included contempt for the intellectual community, particularly the one found in the universities. In the age and community in which he spiritually
belonged, this would not have been an important failure. The
universities had no great political place in the 1920s and
1930s; but in the 1950s and 1960s, they were playing a more
public role. Both Roosevelt and Kennedy had found it useful
to harness elements from the intellectual community to their
administrations. Diefenbaker was unwise to treat the university community with the neglect and contempt that he did. To
take one example – it is difficult to believe that the leading
contemporary theorist of the conservative view of Canadian
history, Professor D.G. Creighton, should never have been

used on the manifold boards, councils, commissions, etc., that formulate our national policies. Not only was he the biographer of Diefenbaker's hero, Sir John A. Macdonald, but Creighton had defined the conservative view of Canada to a whole generation. He had the courage to do this when a definition of conservatism was not being welcomed by the Liberal establishment. Did not Diefenbaker know that the existence of Canada depended on a clear definition of conservatism? Did he not know that there had been diverse formulations of the meaning of Canadian history? For most of his appointments to Royal Commissions and other bodies, Diefenbaker chose the established wealthy or party wheelhorses. When he did choose from the university community, he turned to administrators and technicians, to those with the minimum of intellectual conviction. In the election of 1963, Diefenbaker had no support from the intellectual community, although he was standing on the attractive platform of Canadian sovereignty. This is a measure of how far he had carried yahooism in his years of office. He acted as if friendship with public-relations men and party journalists was a sufficient means to an intellectual nationalism.

Chapter Three

THE DEFENCE CRISIS of 1962 and 1963 revealed the depth of Diefenbaker's nationalism. Except for these events, one might interpret him as a romantic demagogue yearning for recognition. But his actions during the Defence Crisis make it clear that his nationalism was a deeply held principle for which he would fight with great courage and would sacrifice political advantage. Nothing in Diefenbaker's ministry was as noble as his leaving of it. The old war-horse would not budge from his principle: The government of the United States should not be allowed to force the Canadian government to a particular defence policy. His determination to stand on that belief finally convinced the ruling class that he was more than a nuisance, that he must be removed.

One comedy in these tragic events was that the intellectuals could not recognize that Diefenbaker was standing on principle. Such a recognition would have been outside the scope of the class-liberalism by which North-American intellectuals live. The literati had assessed Pearson to be the intellectual of principle who did not know the political arts, and Diefenbaker as the tough provincial politician interested in succeeding at all costs. Yet Diefenbaker was willing to bring the dominant classes of society down on his head; while Pearson changed his defence policies to suit the interests of the powerful. After the Cuban Crisis, Pearson acted with great political skill to unite the powerful forces of continentalism around him.

The crisis over defence blew into an issue after October of 1962, when Kennedy demanded that Castro's Cuba remove its missiles. A conflict had long been brewing between Howard Green, the Minister of External Affairs, and the military, whose spokesman in the Cabinet was Douglas Harkness, the Minister of Defence. It was brought to a head over Cuba because it was rumoured that in the crisis between the United States and the USSR, the Canadian government had been slow in alerting Canadian forces involved in North-American defence. The facts of Canadian action in October of 1962 are still in dispute. It is certainly clear that influential sections of the Canadian military did not think that the government had properly acquiesced in NORAD. The issue soon rose to much greater proportions. Diefenbaker had buzzing around his ears the American government, the military, and soon the uproar of the Canadian power élite with its press. Under Pearson, the Liberal party became the spokesman of these forces. Whether Canada should arm the Bomarc missiles with atomic warheads became the issue at stake. Pearson, who had previously argued that Canada should not accept nuclear arms, turned round and asserted that any government of his would promptly negotiate their acceptance.

The crisis is illuminated by the forces that confronted Diefenbaker during those months. The Canadian head of a great American soap company first questioned publicly the government's relations with the United States. Hellyer and Pearson reversed the Liberal defence policy. The supreme Commander at NATO, General Norstad, gave a press conference in Ottawa under the auspices of the Canadian military, in which he implied that Canada was not living up to its commitments. The American State Department issued a memorandum denying the veracity of the Canadian Prime Minister on the matter. The three Toronto newspapers (two of them traditionally Conservative) came out on the same day for

Diefenbaker's removal. Through all the abuse that Diefenbaker has suffered, he may well remember that it took the full weight of the North-American establishment to bring him down. He may well remember that, in the election of 1963, he still maintained nearly one hundred seats in Parliament when all the resources of the establishment were against him.

In the months of the crisis, there was a clear distinction between the motives of Green and Diefenbaker. They were old and trusted friends, deeply shaped by the same tradition of Canadian conservatism. Green had nominated Diefenbaker for the leadership of his party as long ago as 1948 when George Drew won the contest. When he became Minister of External Affairs in 1959, Green was clearly Diefenbaker's first lieutenant. In this office, his first consideration was that Canada's best role in international affairs should be to use its influence for disarmament. He believed that Canada's acquisition of nuclear arms would add to nuclear tension and diminish Canadian influence abroad. In all this he took for granted that there was such an entity as "Canada," that it was sufficiently a sovereign nation for this kind of policy to be possible. During and after the Cuban Crisis, another factor came more to the fore. Green publicly questioned American actions around the world, not only in Laos and Vietnam. He went as far as to warn the Americans that their preponderant power might tempt them to be bullies. Indeed, in those months he expressed a deeper disquiet about the role of the United States in the world than any Canadian leader had done for generations. In Parliament, on January 24, 1963, he said:

The Cuban episode has made perfectly clear that in the world today the preponderance of power is with the United States. No longer is it a question of two great equal nuclear powers.

I suggest that at the present time the United States is beyond any shadow of doubt preponderant in power. That, Mr. Chairman, may constitute quite a temptation. When you are the biggest fellow in the school yard it is quite a temptation to shove everybody else around. Now, I am confident that there will be no such development in United States policy. I am confident that they will not adopt a policy of getting tough with their allies. For Canada, of course, it is particularly important whether anything of that kind develops.[6]

Whether he was wise to be so explicit depends on how one interprets the role of the United States in the world, and this question cannot be undertaken here. Suffice it to say that for those who accept Howard Green's interpretation, his actions during those months make him one of the rare politicians who literally deserve the prefix "Right Honourable." Whether wisely or not, Canada played a more independent role internationally during those short months than ever before in its history. It was not likely that the American government under Kennedy would take such talk lightly from its closest "ally." The gentler régime of Eisenhower was a thing of the past. In 1962, Kennedy had made clear that the United States was no longer going to take any nonsense from its allies. An air of innocence pervades Green's statements about the United States. He spoke as if his comments would be taken in friendship. He seemed unaware that he was an official in a satellite country. Can an ant be an ally with an elephant?

Diefenbaker stood for a much more limited nationalism. He did not criticize American world policy, but insisted that Canadian defence policy should not be determined in Washington. Only at one point did he by implication criticize American

6   See *Hansard* of that date, 3067.

world policy. In calling for the UN to investigate Cuba, he
implied that he did not automatically accept Kennedy's account
of the facts. At no other time did he imply any criticism of
America's world role; he simply affirmed his belief in Canadian
sovereignty. In his speech to Parliament on February 5, 1963,
just before it voted down his government – surely a great doc-
ument of Canadian nationalism – he did not attack American
policy even when the weight of the American government was
being used against him through General Norstad's press conference and the press release on Canadian relations by the
American State Department.[7] Even during the following election, when he was under attack by such friends of the
Kennedys as the publisher of *Newsweek*, and when the Liberals had the Kennedys' own election expert Louis Harris advis-
ing them, he refrained from any attack on the aims of the
American Empire. He continually repeated that Canada
should settle its defence commitments after the facts were clar-
ified by the NATO meetings in May of 1963. His opponents
successfully raised the cry of "indecisiveness." (Decisiveness
had become a good slogan under the Kennedys.) They
explained his actions by saying that he was trying to have the

7 On his first trip abroad, after his Inauguration in 1961, Kennedy
   had come to Ottawa and made a strong pitch for Canada's membership in the OAS, which was met without response from the Canadian
   government and Parliament. The President had also publicly
   announced that the United States was going to demand greater
   cooperation from its "allies," even if this meant less ease in friendship. In light of these events, it is surprising how Diefenbaker
   showed himself little ready for the great pressure that the American
   government would exert for the overthrow of his regime. Because
   of his early assassination, Kennedy's policy of exerting pressure on
   his "allies" only succeeded with two countries, Canada and the
   United Kingdom.

best of Harkness's and Green's positions for the low motive of
political success. Such an explanation cannot hold water for
the simple reason that he was willing to let Harkness go, and
in doing so he must have known the price he was paying. His
speech at the dissolution of parliament made clear that the one
thing he would not stomach was the United States government
determining Canadian defence policy.

Diefenbaker and General Pearkes, the Defence Minister
before Harkness, had negotiated the acceptance of the
Bomarcs when they scrapped the Arrow program. The
Bomarcs were useless without nuclear warheads. It was
claimed that in refusing the warheads Diefenbaker was reneg-
ing on his own commitment to the United States. It was even
claimed that he might not have understood the nature of the
original commitment. In refusing to make up his mind about
accepting the warheads, he was accused of being "indecisive."
The "bad ally" and "the man of indecision" became Liberal
images for the campaign.

Diefenbaker answered these charges in his speech to Parliament on January 25, 1963.[8] He claimed that the acceptance of warheads for the Bomarcs had always been
conditional on needing them for the defence of the alliance.
Defence technology was in constant flux, and it was no
longer clear that warheads were necessary. He maintained
that the decision should await the NATO meetings in May of
1963, when there was to be an over-all assessment of the military needs of the alliance. The interests of world peace
demanded that warheads should be kept off Canadian soil
until it was certain that they were needed. This speech illu-
minates his assumptions about Canada's place in the world.

---

8 It will be well for historians to read the *Hansard* of that day. By this
stage in the crisis, the press was baying for Diefenbaker's blood, so
the force of his arguments was not given much public prominence.

He was no pacifist, no unilateralist, nor was he sentimental about Communism. If nuclear arms were necessary for North-American defence, Canada would take them. He also assumed that NATO was an alliance and not simply an American instrument. (After all, it was the Russians who had maintained the contrary for many years.) Canada's sovereignty entailed that our defence policy be determined in Ottawa. These last two assumptions did not correspond with reality and could not be politically sustained in the climate of Diefenbaker's own country.

How much was Diefenbaker aware that Canadian nationalism was no longer an effective rallying-cry in the urban Canada of 1963? Did a man with his past realize how much the structure of society had been changed in the Howe era so that the ruling class was no longer indigenous? Was he aware that a branch-plant society could not possibly show independence over an issue on which the American government was seriously determined? Most Canadians were as convinced as the American public that Kennedy had been right doing what he did in Cuba, and that his actions showed the wisdom of "decisiveness" in foreign policy. So "decisiveness" was subtly identified with Canada's need to have atomic arms.

Green's appeal to a gentler tradition of international morality had little attraction for the new Canada, outside of such unimportant groups as the Voice of Women. It seems likely that Diefenbaker actually believed that NATO was an alliance of sovereign states, not an instrument of the American Empire. Pearson had always acted internationally from different premises. His unequivocal praise of American action in Cuba showed that he knew there was a difference between Canadian initiative limiting the actions of a dying British power at the time of Suez and Canadian influence limiting the actions of the American Empire. He could use the rhetoric of "internationalism" even more effectively than Green, but he knew it for what it was.

Can it be denied that the actions of the Kennedy administration were directed toward removing an unreliable government in Ottawa rather than to guaranteeing a specific
commitment? The American Secretary of Defense, Robert
McNamara, made clear that the Bomarcs were not essential to
the defence of North America. Diefenbaker and Green must
have seemed too suspicious of American motives to be allowed
to remain in office.[9] Their relation to the OAS and Cuba endan-
gered what lay ahead in South America. Kennedy was a past
master in the use of power for personal and imperial purposes.
Historians will only be able to speculate about what Pearson
and Kennedy discussed before the dinner for Nobel-Prize win-
ners at the White House in 1962.

The Defence Crisis illustrated how profoundly Diefenbaker's Canadianism was bound up with the British connection. Since 1914, Britain had ceased to be a great power. Both
Green and Diefenbaker continued to accept as real, however,
the meaning of Canada's membership in the British Commonwealth. The character of Canada as British North America
was in their flesh and bones. Yet it was their fate to be in
charge of the Canadian government at the time that the English ruling class had come to think of its Commonwealth relations as a tiresome burden, when the wealthy of Canada had
ceased to be connected with their British past. It is easy for the
clever and the rootless to point out the mistakes that Diefenbaker and Green made in this regard; it is kinder, however, to
sympathize with these men of deep loyalty, who found themselves impotent in the face of their disappearing past.

The British connection had been a source of Canadian
nationalism. The west-east pull of trade – from the prairies,

9 In the election of 1963, American officials followed Green to his
   political meetings. It was innocent of Green to object to this. Did he
   not know how the CIA considered South American elections?

economic

political philosophy

down the Great Lakes and the St. Lawrence, to western Europe – provided a counter-thrust to the pull of continentalism. It depended on the existence of a true North Atlantic triangle. But the Britishness of Canada was more than economic. It was a tradition that stood in firm opposition to the Jeffersonian liberalism so dominant in the United States.[10] By its nature this conservatism was not philosophically explicit, although it had shaped our institutions and had penetrated into the lives of generations of Canadians. Green and Diefenbaker were of this tradition. Such Canadians could not give their loyalty to the great Republic to the south. This did not imply anti-Americanism, simply a lack of Americanism. In the election of 1963, Diefenbaker was accused of anti-Americanism, but he was surely being honest to his own past when he said that he thought of his policies as being pro-Canadian, not anti-American. During the Howe era, this older Canadianism disappeared first in Toronto and Montreal, cities that once prided themselves on being most British. But ways of life die hard, and this loyalty still survived in the less modern parts of Canada. Loyalty cannot quickly be destroyed by economic circumstances because it does not depend on economics alone. In his speech at dissolution in 1963, Diefenbaker spoke with unerring historical appropriateness when he reminded his hearers of the Annexation Manifesto of 1849. The economic self-seekers had never been the ones to care about Canada as a nation.

With his passionate sense of British North America, Diefenbaker took office at a time when the Suez venture had driven home to the English their exact place in the world. The British decided then that their hope for any international influence lay in a careful manipulation of their "special" relation with the

10 A discussion of British conservatism will be found later.

United States.[11] The loan that Keynes negotiated for them after 1945 guaranteed their being tied to the American Empire. Whether or not there was any alternative, they saw none. After all, their greatest contemporary leader, Churchill, had not de Gaulle's clarity of intelligence. Beginning in the 1960s, the United Kingdom decided to seek entrance to the new European community. They saw the European Common Market as an outreach of American power. They desired to _British_ free themselves as gracefully as possible from Commonwealth commitments. The length to which the English were willing to carry their "special" relation was seen in Lord Hume's trumpeting of support for American policy in Cuba, and Mr. Macmillan's ability to eat crow when the Americans cancelled the Skybolt program. As realistic a politician as de Gaulle graphically described the English as a Trojan Horse when he vetoed their entrance to Europe in January of 1963.

In this context, the appeal of the Conservatives to the British connection carried an air of unreality. The pattern of Canadian trade could not be changed in the way Diefenbaker suggested in 1957. He understood this himself by the time he turned down the United Kingdom's later proposals for a free-trade area with Canada. After such a refusal, the English could not stomach the appeal he made for the Commonwealth in London, in September of 1962. It seemed the stuff of fantasy, not a viable alternative. Tough politicians like Macmillan and Duncan Sandys were quick to use the press, and Diefenbaker was accused of trying to upset England's entry into the Common Market. Men who felt deeply about the Commonwealth could be accused of being bad allies, not

11 Bismarck said the central fact of the modern era was that the Americans spoke English. In 1917, the English brought in the Americans to settle their European quarrel. Thirty years later their ally had become their master.

only of the United States but also of the United Kingdom. The two had become synonymous, once the English had become a satellite. This was made crystal clear when Lord Home welcomed Pearson back to power as a "good ally" at the NATO meetings in Ottawa in May of 1963. Because the English had been rejected by the Europeans as an American Trojan Horse, they had little sympathy with such a peripheral matter as Canadian nationalism. After what the English did to him in 1962 and 1963, Diefenbaker still fought for the Red Ensign in 1964. His basic principles were far removed from any petty sense of self-importance.

It was often considered strange that a Conservative government should follow the independent internationalism associated with Green. The only explanation brought forward by its opponents was that the administration was overwhelmed with a pathological "indecision." But there was something consistent and inevitable in Green's policies. Green and Diefenbaker had always considered Canada an independent country. The role of Canada was to mediate between the United States and western Europe, particularly Great Britain. But this conception could no longer fit the facts. By the 1950s NATO was a servant of the American Empire. The Canadian élite accepted the consequences of this for Canada. But Green could not accept the end of independence. He cried out against Canada becoming a vassal. As the Commonwealth had so little substance, the only role now possible seemed that of an independent agent in the United Nations, exerting influence for disarmament. His Protestant idealism pointed in the same direction. But such independence in international relations was not something the dominant forces in Canadian life could accept. The sincerity of Diefenbaker's nationalism is established by the fact that he stood by Green, and would not accept the American demands, even when it was in his overwhelming interest to do so. One is reminded of Milton's Abdiel: "Unshaken, unseduced, unterrified."

Chapter Four

IN THE LIGHT OF DIEFENBAKER, I would like to turn to the Canadian establishment and its political instrument, the Liberal party. There are three arguments for nationalism that could justify the Liberals. First, the Liberals are the realistic defenders of this country, piloting us through the shoals of foreign control and internal dissension that might shipwreck Canada. Second, in the twentieth century it is inevitable that Canada should be swallowed up; since 1940 this should have been obvious to any political analyst. Liberal leadership has recognized this and has taught the masses to accept it smoothly. Third, Canada's disappearance is not only necessary but good. As part of the great North American civilization, we enter wider horizons; Liberal policies are leading to a richer continentalism. The second and third arguments are often taken to be the same. They are identified because men assume in the age of progress that the broad movement of history is upward. Taken as a whole, what is bound to happen is bound also to be good. But this assumption is not self-evident. The fact that events happen does not imply that they are good. We understand this in the small events of personal life. We only forget it in the large events when we worship the future. The last two arguments for the Liberals are, therefore, clearly distinct.

The Liberals use the first of these three in public. There is still much nationalist sentiment in certain parts of the country. On the hustings the image of the Liberals has been that of the realistic defenders of Canadian unity. At the level of economic

Liberals

Libs

liberal reasoning ↓ economic policies

policy, the argument runs, they have shown themselves skilful masters of national development. This skill was exemplified in the policies of Howe from 1945 to 1957. These policies proceeded from the recognition of certain realities: that the Canadian economy was part of the total resources of North America; that Canada was an undeveloped frontier within that total, and the capital necessary for that development would come largely from the United States; that North America was committed to a capitalist structure in which the control of production would be in the hands of "private" corporations, while the government would only play a supervisory role.

Within these assumptions, the Liberal party gave brilliant leadership to the development of the country; the corporations ran an economy that was blessed by a benevolent government; certain complementary needs were met by the judicious use of Crown corporations; injustices were palliated with limited social services. If the terms for American investment had been tougher, there would have been less investment. Canada would have developed more slowly and with a substantially lower standard of living than the United States. This would have been the quickest way to undermine the nation. The inevitability of Howe's policies is seen by the fact that the Conservatives could find no viable alternative. Since coming back to office in 1963, the Liberals have recognized the need for a more nationalistic economic policy. Only the circumstances of minority government have prevented Walter Gordon from initiating it.

Qc

Beyond economic policy, the argument continues, the Liberals alone have understood that French Canada is the keystone of Confederation. They have always allowed for the legitimate interests of Quebec and have produced French leaders who supported Confederation. The provincial Liberal party has directed Quebec's awakening since Duplessis, and from 1963 the federal party has recognized that Quebec must have a new place in Confederation, if it is going to remain in the same country. Co-operative federalism is the only basis on which Quebec will stay. Pearson has wisely compromised with Prime Minister Lesage on matters of provincial autonomy. He has fought for a national flag free of any hated British symbols. He has established a strong Royal Commission on Bilingualism and Biculturalism. When one compares this with the previous administration, the claim of the Liberals is strong.

At the level of defence policy, the Liberals argue that the issue about nuclear arms did not involve any surrender of proper Canadian sovereignty. Canada ought to play a fair and honourable part in "the defence of the West," and the Americans are the leaders of that alliance. It is only in terms of such realities that our nation can be built. Only as a friendly satellite of the United States can we use such diplomats as Pearson to influence the American leaders to play their world role with skill and moderation. Doing this is not negating nationalism but recognizing its limits. The Liberal argument was symbolized in August of 1963 when, on the same weekend that the secret agreement with the United States over nuclear warheads was announced, Pearson spoke feelingly about Canadian nationalism at a meeting of Quebec journalists.

The whole argument for the Liberals as realistic nationalists breaks down with their actual achievements. Their policies have not been such as could sustain a continuing nation. The old adage "The operation was a success but the patient died" can be too readily applied. They were in office during the years when the possible basis for nationalism disappeared. It was under a Liberal régime that Canada became a branch-plant society; it was under Liberal leadership that our independence in defence and foreign affairs was finally broken. It is perfectly convincing to argue that these policies were necessary for Canada or to argue that they were good for Canada. The widespread claim that the Liberals were the best possible régime is not the issue at this point. It may be convincing to argue that if Howe had not existed, we would have had to invent him. But it is absurd to argue that the Liberals have been successful nationalists.

The Liberals failed in English-speaking Canada. If the nation were to survive, it had to be anchored in both English- and French-speaking Canada, and a *modus vivendi* had to be established between the two. The Liberals failed to recognize that the real danger to nationalism lay in the incipient continentalism of English-speaking society, rather than in any Quebec separatism. Their economic policies homogenized the culture of Ontario with that of Michigan and New York.

The crucial years were those of the early forties. The decisions of those years were made once and for all, and were not compatible with the continuance of a sovereign Canadian nation.[12] Once it was decided that Canada was to be a branch-plant society of American capitalism, the issue of Canadian nationalism had been settled. The decision may or may not have been necessary; it may have been good or bad for Canada to be integrated into the international capitalism that has dominated the West since 1945. But certainly Canada could not exist as a nation when the chief end of the government's policy was the quickest integration into that complex. The Liberal policy under Howe was integration as fast as possible and at all costs. No other consideration was allowed to stand in the

12 A note is required here about the use of such words as "decision" and "possible." In writing history one employs a certain logic, which one hopes has a high degree of consistency. For example, the use of the word "decisions" does not entail any concept of free will or imply that these "decisions" "could have been otherwise." It is clear that in this writing I am employing the word "fate" in a way that most modern writers avoid. They accept a modern notion of free will, while I accept a classical account of ethics. In this writing I cannot justify that vocabulary.

way. The society produced by such policies may reap enormous benefits, but it will not be a nation. Its culture will become the empire's to which it belongs. Branch-plant economies have branch-plant cultures. The O'Keefe Centre symbolizes Canada.

The Ontario vote in the national election of 1963 showed what that society had become. In the southern metropolitan areas, the writ of the continental corporations runs with small impediment, and the Liberals swept the board. A society dominated by corporations could not vote for an independent defence policy. The power of the American government to control Canada does not lie primarily in its ability to exert direct pressure; the power lies in the fact that the dominant classes in Canada see themselves at one with the continent on all essential matters. Dominant classes get the kind of government they want. The nature of our rulers was determined by the economic policies of the Liberals in the 1940s. The matter can be summed up quickly: The policies pursued by Howe produced a ruling class composed of such men as E.P. Taylor. In the winter of 1963, Mr. Taylor was quoted as saying: "Canadian nationalism! How old-fashioned can you get?"

The democratic argument asserts that it took more votes than the votes of the powerful to make Pearson Prime Minister. Was it not the majority of Canadian people – and not simply the managers – that settled the issue? To meet this argument would require a long account of corporation capitalism and the processes whereby power is legitimized. This can obviously not be done in a short space. Let it suffice to make the following point: In no society is it possible for many men to live outside the dominant assumptions of their world for very long. Where can people learn independent views, when newspapers and television throw at them only processed opinions? In a society of large bureaucracies, power is legitimized by conscious and unconscious processes. The overwhelming vote for the Liberals in urban Ontario should not be surprising, since the powers of legitimacy were naturally strongest in those areas controlled by continental capitalism. The democratic idea of the free man making up his mind to create the society of his choice as he casts his ballot may have had meaning at some moments in history, but it can hardly apply in as dynamic a society as Southern Ontario. To say this is not to deny that the ballot box has ritual and other significance. A society proceeding from economic decisions made in the forties was not one capable of deciding on a defence policy or a foreign policy different from those of the United States or, for that matter, deciding on a distinct culture. Ontario was determined it would be integrated into the Great Lakes region.

It has been said that the inability of a country to have an independent foreign policy does not prevent it from being a nation. This means that Canadians have to recognize the limitations on sovereignty in a nation that lives beside the most powerful country on earth. This argument sees our case as similar to that of Poland. But whatever possible future there may be for Poland, there are clearly two chief differences between ourselves and that nation. First, the Poles have an ancient culture which has shown strength in resisting the new change. The new came to Poland not only as something Russian (that is, nationally alien) but also as something Marxist (that is, profoundly alien to a Roman Catholic people). In Canada outside of Quebec, there is no deeply rooted culture, and the new changes come in the form of an ideology (capitalist and liberal) which seems to many a splendid vision of human existence. Second, we are different from Poland in that in many ways capitalist imperialism is much harder to resist than Communist imperialism. This is not simply a matter of counting up the Hungarys and Tibets, the Brazils and Guatemalas, and seeing which empire has the lowest score. Nor is it simply that the United States is the most progressive society on earth and therefore the most radical force for the homogenizing of the world. By its very nature the capitalist system makes of national boundaries only matters of political formality. The governments of small capitalist nations do not have the same means to protect themselves as do small Communist states. Economic control is not finally in the hands of the government, and foreign capital is able to determine possible governments by incarnating itself as an indigenous ruling class. When Pearson praised Howe at the Liberal convention of 1958, he was surely showing that the existence of the Canadian nation was not a priority on the agenda of the Liberal party. The one implies the other.

Whether or not Pearson intended or recognized this implication is fundamentally unimportant. I do not wish to impugn the motives of the Liberal leaders. To understand public events, it is necessary to distinguish between "decision" and "intention." Intention, political or otherwise, is always hard to fathom. This does not prevent decisions made in public having consequences that are not difficult to understand. The "personalized" political journalism, associated on this continent with *Time* and exemplified in Canada by *Maclean's*, has done much to obscure this fundamental distinction. In the preceding arguments I am not concerned with the nature of intention, but with that of decision. It is therefore unnecessary to discuss whether those responsible were aware of the likely results of their decisions, or whether they thought these consequences good. For example, nothing that has been said implies that Pearson or his lieutenant, Jack Pickersgill, did not think of themselves as nationalists. To speculate about the intentions of those who were responsible for these decisions would require a series of biographies. One man might be described as believing in continentalism but as using the rhetoric of nationalism as the necessary cloak of the politician; another might be explained to be a nationalist who nevertheless could not bear to be out of office; a third might be a nationalist who did not understand the consequences of what he voted for in Cabinet. The results would not much affect the issues. The consequences of decisions can be understood historically for what they are, whereas the motives of the decision-makers are mainly of biographical – and perhaps of eternal – significance. Biography is not the purpose of this writing. The assertion that the Liberals were not successful nationalists does not depend on any assessment of their characters.[13]

The second way to justify the Liberals is to argue that politics is the art of leading people to accept necessities. As the argument goes, it was necessary for Canada to become part of the civilization of the United States. The Liberals have been the smooth instrument of that necessity. The last part of this argument has already been accepted – Liberal policies have led efficiently in that direction. Their record of smoothness is marred by their defeat in 1957. But they have quickly and efficiently regained power. The argument then turns on the truth of its first proposition, whether or not it was necessary for Canada to become part of the homogenized continental culture. And this in turn hinges on the question whether there were any possible alternatives to the decisions taken in the 1940s. If there were none, the necessity of Canada's disappearance is plain, and the argument in favour of the Liberal party follows.

13 The large amount of biographical writing about Mackenzie King in the last decade has done little to elucidate to what degree he was a nationalist, a continentalist, a man chiefly concerned about office, or a subtle conglomeration of all three, held together by his belief that a brilliant manipulation of day-to-day events was in his ordained hands sufficient to bring about the best of all possible worlds. King's biographers have failed to elucidate his intentions, partly because they did not understand what Marx and Freud have taught us about the logic of "intention."

What would these alternative policies have been? Nations must resist the capitalist and Communist empires in different ways. Resistance to western imperialism has taken two main forms. The first is to establish a rigorous socialist state that turns to the Communist empire for support in maintaining itself. This policy can be called Castroism after its most successful practitioner. The second method is to harness the nationalist spirit to technological planning and to insist internationally that there are limits to the western "alliance." This policy may be called Gaullism after its most successful practitioner.

Castroism was so obviously not a possible policy for Canada in the middle forties that it is hardly worth making the point that it was not. "Leftist" nationalism is only possible in a less-developed society in which the majority of citizens desires industrialism and believes that this is being prevented by anti-nationalist forces from the capitalist empire. This was not the situation in Canada.[14] Was there the possibility of some form of Gaullism in which the planning and control of investment would have left the ordering of the economy in Canadian hands? Gaullism is only possible when nationalism is such a dominant motive among certain élites that they are able to control the economy so as to stop the tendency of

14 Could Canada have achieved even the degree of independence that Mexico has maintained? This is not the place to compare the complex differences between the two countries. The conflict between the Spanish and the Indian in Mexico allowed the country to fit incomparably less easily into the common western pattern. Can one imagine Canadians expropriating the oil properties and taking on international capitalism as Cardenas did in the 1930s? Even with these traditions, it would seem likely that as Mexico is industrialized, its new middle class will make it an increasingly acquiescent neighbour.

capitalism to become international. There are no such élites in
the Canada of 1965.

In an earlier era) Macdonald's "National Policy" was of the
Gaullist kind. It was possible because enough Canadians were
determined to pay the economic price for such nationalism,
and because Britain was still a dominant force pulling the flow
of trade eastward. Enough entrepreneurs could resist the pull
of continentalism. Since R.B. Bennett's abortive social legislation of the late thirties, and the acquiescence of the succeeding
Liberal government, the business community (particularly in
Montreal, which was then more important than Toronto) has
identified its interests with the Liberal party. This was
Mackenzie King's chief political achievement. The organization of the war and of postwar reconstruction was carried on
within the assumption that government action never questioned the ultimate authority of business interests to run the
economy. Howe's cost-plus arrangements for war production
make this clear. The Liberal politicians and civil servants
always acted within that assumption because they knew their
limited power depended on it. No government that acted on
other principles would have lasted long. And to repeat, after
1940 it was not in the interests of the economically powerful
to be nationalists. Most of them made more money by being
the representatives of American capitalism and setting up the
branch plants. No class in Canada more welcomed the American managers than the established wealthy of Montreal and
Toronto, who had once seen themselves the pillars of Canada.
Nor should this be surprising. Capitalism is, after all, a way of
life based on the principle that the most important activity is
profit-making. That activity led the wealthy in the direction of
continentalism. They lost nothing essential to the principle of
their lives in losing their country. It is this very fact that has
made capitalism the great solvent of all tradition in the modern era. When everything is made relative to profit-making, all

traditions of virtue are dissolved, including that aspect of virtue known as love of country. This is why liberalism is the perfect ideology for capitalism. It demolishes those taboos that restrain expansion. Even the finest talk about internationalism opens markets for the powerful.

If there had been an influential group that seriously desired the continuance of the country after 1940, it would have needed the animation of some political creed that differed from the capitalist liberalism of the United States. Only then could they have acted with sufficient decision to build an alternative nation on this continent. De Gaulle has been able to count on a deeply felt nationalism. This is based on a tradition that pre-dates the age of progress and yet is held by men who can handle the modern world. But no such tradition existed among any of the important decision-makers in Canada. The only Canadians who had a profoundly different tradition from capitalist liberalism were the French Canadians, and they were not generally taken into decision making unless they had foregone these traditions. Their very Catholicism did not lead the best of them to be interested in the managerial, financial, and technical skills of the age of progress.

The only possible basis for a Gaullist élite would have been the senior civil servants working closely with politicians who knew what they were doing. Such a union of civil servants and politicians could have used the power of Ottawa to control the representatives of continentalism in Toronto and Montreal. In fact, the Liberal politicians and their civil servants saw themselves in pleasant co-operation with the tycoons of the real capitals. I must repeat again Mackenzie King's great discovery: If his government was the friend of business, the Liberal party could stay in office almost indefinitely. His chosen representative for that co-operation was C.D. Howe. An old newspaper photograph lingers in the mind. In the summer of 1945, a crowd of strikers followed Howe to a Toronto golf club. They had not been allowed to reach the Minister of Trade and Commerce officially. He was forced to speak with the unionists to get them out of the locker room. In his anger at the invasion of the country club, Howe made perfectly plain what post-war reconstruction would be like. The continental corporations were going to rule. Such Liberal politicians as Brooke Claxton and Paul Martin knew where the real power lay – in St. James and Bay Streets. They did not risk using the government as a nationalist instrument. The politicians, the businessmen, and the civil servants worked harmoniously together. The enormous majorities for the Liberals in 1945, 1948, and 1953 showed that the Canadian people were attuned to the system produced by this co-operation.

Any desire for nationalism among the civil service could not be effective. Some of them who directly served Howe, like Mitchell Sharp and William Bennett, obviously welcomed the union between government and international business. When they were forced out of the government by the Conservatives in 1958, they quickly found high places in international companies. But what of the traditional civil servants in the Departments of Finance and External Affairs? They had given their lives to government service and presumably wanted to serve a sovereign Canada. For over a generation, choruses of praise have been offered to these civil servants. How wonderful for Canada that it should be represented by such permanent officials as Norman Robertson and Robert Bryce. They have been spoken of as a kind of secular priesthood. Yet the country they represented is now a fragmented nation, a satellite.

It would be a travesty to deny that most of them wanted to preserve their country. But they were not of the diamond stuff of which nationalists must be made in these circumstances. Their education was not of a kind to produce a realistic attitude toward the twentieth century. The officials of the Department of Finance had mostly learnt their economics at Queen's

University in Ontario, where the glories of the free market were the first dogma. But nationalism was negated by the policies that proceeded from such a dogma. The officials of External Affairs had mostly been educated in the twilight scepticism of Oxford liberalism. This kind of culture does not give one the stamina to be a nationalist in the twentieth century. They went on representing Canada at significant conferences, while the "new" Canada was being shaped by other hands in Southern Ontario. The old-fashioned city of Ottawa continued to shelter them from the Canada they had helped to make. They were not in a position to be the necessary nationalist élite. But where else could it come from? Isolated intellectuals in the universities? Small-town politicians who remembered?

Nevertheless it is interesting to speculate why the civil service élite did so little. To take the example of one government department, it seems likely that some officials in External Affairs have some feeling for the continuance of their nation. Yet they were the instruments of a policy that left Canada a satellite internationally. In 1940, it was necessary for Canada to throw in her lot with continental defence. The whole of Eurasia might have fallen into the hands of Germany and Japan. The British Empire was collapsing once and for all as an international force. Canada and the United States of America had to be unequivocally united for the defence of this hemisphere. But it is surprising how little the politicians and officials seem to have realized that this new situation would have to be manipulated with great wisdom if any Canadian independence was to survive. Perhaps nothing could have been done; perhaps the collapse of nineteenth-century Europe automatically entailed the collapse of Canada. Nevertheless, it is extraordinary that King and his associates in External Affairs did not seem to recognize the perilous situation that the new circumstances entailed. In all eras, wise politicians have to play a balancing game. How little the American alliance was balanced by any defence of national independence!

In the case of King, this lack of balance seems to be bound up with a very usual syndrome among people who give themselves to the practical life: when they gain power they carry on with the ideas they learnt thirty years before. King had seen the centre of Canadian independence as being threatened by the British; he had been raised by a beloved mother who was impregnated with the memory of the supposed injustices that her father, William Lyon Mackenzie, had received at the hands of the British. Even after 1940, he still held the fear that Canadian independence was threatened from Whitehall. It may also have been that King was sufficiently held by liberal theory to believe that the United States was a democracy, and therefore not in essence an imperial power like the old societies of Europe. His relations with the Rockefellers were certainly a classic case of the ability of liberals to fool themselves about the relation between capitalism and democracy. King seems to have admired instinctively the liberal rhetoric of Franklin Delano Roosevelt, and Roosevelt surely stands as a perfect example of the division between ideology and action. One of the great imperialists of American history imagined himself an enemy of imperialism.

In the late forties, NATO policy seems to have been advocated by senior civil servants not only as defence against the Russian Empire but also as a means of building an Atlantic community that would provide tugs on Canada other than the continental. Yet by the 1960s, NATO had become the military instrument of the strongest empire on earth. It may indeed be argued that the safety of the western world against the hostile forces of Asia requires that we be part of a tightly unified empire; the integration of Canada into that empire would be a small price to pay. Yet as realistic a politician as de Gaulle recognizes that he must try to limit the power of NATO if the existence of France as a country is to be maintained. American hegemony was obvious. Why was it not balanced by a greater initiative for independence? In the Defence Crisis of 1963, Green and Diefenbaker did not receive loyalty from their civil service. General Norstad's press conference in Ottawa in January of 1963 could hardly have been organized without help – the help of various top officials in the very government that held the policies that Norstad's remarks were undermining. Presumably the permanent officials felt justified in this action because their view of Canada was entirely dominated by the concept of "the good ally."

What seems central to this process is that such officials had in the previous twenty years become more and more representative of a western empire rather than civil servants of a particular nation state. They were part of an international bureaucracy, mainly English-speaking, whose chief job was to see that the West maintained its superior power over the East. They identified themselves with the international community rather than with nationalist "hayseeds" such as Green and Diefenbaker. In the final analysis, they were provincial servants of the greatest empire since Rome. Was there anything that could have been done to preserve Canadian independence after 1960? Where were the people in Canada who could have done it?

Chapter Five

THE CONFUSED STRIVINGS of politicians, businessmen, and civil servants cannot alone account for Canada's collapse. This stems from the very character of the modern era.[15] The aspirations of progress have made Canada redundant. The universal and homogeneous state is the pinnacle of political striving. "Universal" implies a world-wide state, which would eliminate the curse of war among nations; "homogeneous" means that all men would be equal, and war among classes would be eliminated. The masses and the philosophers have both agreed that this universal and egalitarian society is the goal of historical striving. It gives content to the rhetoric of both Communists and capitalists. This state will be achieved by means of modern science – a science that leads to the conquest of nature. Today scientists master not only non-human nature, but human nature itself. Particularly in America, scientists concern themselves with the control of heredity, the human mind, and society. Their victories in biochemistry and psychology will give the politicians a prodigious power to universalize and homogenize. Since 1945, the world-wide and

15 In what follows I use "modern" to describe the civilization of the age of progress. This civilization arose in Western Europe and is now conquering the whole globe and perhaps other parts of the universe. "Modern" is applied to political philosophy to distinguish the thought of Western Europe from that of the antique world of Greece.

uniform society is no longer a distant dream but a close possibility. Man will conquer man and perfect himself.

Modern civilization makes all local cultures anachronistic. Where modern science has achieved its mastery, there is no place for local cultures. It has often been argued that geography and language caused Canada's defeat. But behind these there is a necessity that is incomparably more powerful. Our culture floundered on the aspirations of the age of progress. The argument that Canada, a local culture, must disappear can, therefore, be stated in three steps. First, men everywhere move ineluctably toward membership in the universal and homogeneous state. Second, Canadians live next to a society that is the heart of modernity. Third, nearly all Canadians think that modernity is good, so nothing essential distinguishes Canadians from Americans. When they oblate themselves before "the American way of life," they offer themselves on the altar of the reigning Western goddess. When Pearson set out on his electoral campaign of 1963, he was photographed reading Will Durant's *The Dawning of the Age of Reason*. To Durant, the age of reason is the age of progress. The book was therefore appropriate reading for Pearson, who was about to persuade Canadians to adopt American atomic arms.

There are many who would deny the second statement in the previous paragraph, that the United States is the spearhead of progress. Strangely enough, the two groups that deny it do so from opposite positions. The Marxists deny it from progressive assumptions, and American "conservatives" deny it because they consider their country the chief guardian of Western values. These two points of view are sometimes confused and combined by certain Europeans whose jealousy of the United States leads them to accuse Americans of being too reactionary and too modern at one and the same time. To maintain my stand that the United States is the spearhead of progress, these two denials must be refuted. To do so, I must turn away from Canadian history to the more important questions of modern political theory. Marxists believe that their philosophy leads to the true understanding of history. They insist that the aims of the United States are hostile to the interests of developing humanity. They assert that American corporation capitalism – its system of property relations and consequent world policies – makes the United States an essentially "reactionary" rather than a "progressive" force. The Russian and Chinese leaders may disagree on how to deal with this situation, but they do not disagree about the diagnosis. Canadian Marxists have therefore argued that Canadian nationalism serves the interests of progress because our incorporation in the United States would add to the power of reaction in the world. To be progressive in Canada is to be nationalistic. To see where the Marxists are wrong in detail about Canada, I must discuss where they are wrong about the age of progress in general.

Marxism

Marx believed that history unfolds as progress, and that when man's control of nature has eliminated scarcity, the objective conditions will be present for a society in which human beings no longer exploit each other. With the end of exploitation, men will not be alienated from their own happiness or from each other. A society will emerge in which the full claims of personal freedom and social order will be reconciled, because the essential cause of conflict between men will have been overcome. This world-wide society will be one in which all human beings can at last realize their happiness in the world without the necessity of lessening that of others. This doctrine implies that there are ways of life in which men are fulfilled and others in which they are not. How else could Marx distinguish between man's alienation and its opposite? Marxism includes therefore a doctrine of human good (call it, if you will, happiness). Technological development is a means by which all men will realize this good. But such a doctrine of good means that Marx is not purely a philosopher of the age of progress; he is rooted in the teleological philosophy that pre-dates the age of progress. It is the very signature of mod-ern man to deny reality to any conception of good that imposes limits on human freedom. To modern political theory, man's essence is his freedom. Nothing must stand in the way of our absolute freedom to create the world as we want it. There must be no conceptions of good that put limitations on human action. This definition of man as freedom constitutes the heart of the age of progress. The doctrine of progress is not, as Marx believed, the perfectibility of man, but an open-ended progression in which men will be endlessly free to make the world as they want it. In Marxism, technology remains an instrument that serves human good. But many technologists speak as if mastery were an end in itself. To conquer space it may be necessary to transcend ordinary humanity, and produce creatures half flesh and half metal.

North-American liberalism expresses the belief in open-ended progress more accurately than Marxism. It understands more fully the implications of man's essence being his freedom. As liberals become more and more aware of the implications of their own doctrine, they recognize that no appeal to human good, now or in the future, must be allowed to limit their freedom to make the world as they choose. Social order is a man-made convenience, and its only purpose is to increase freedom. What matters is that men shall be able to do what they want, when they want. The logic of this liberalism makes the distinction between judgements of fact and judgements of value. "Value judgements" are subjective. In other words, man in his freedom creates the valuable. The human good is what we choose for our good.

In an earlier generation, liberals such as John Dewey claimed that this doctrine improved upon the past because it guaranteed a society in which all could do what they wanted, in which the standards of some would not be imposed upon others. Tastes are different, and we should have a society that caters to the plurality of tastes. How much fairer this would be than the old societies in which standards of virtue were imposed on the masses by pertinacious priests and arrogant philosophers. But this is not what is happening in our state capitalism. In the private spheres, all kinds of tastes are allowed. Nobody minds very much if we prefer women or dogs or boys, as long as we cause no public inconvenience. But in the public sphere, such pluralism of taste is not permitted. The conquest of human and nonhuman nature becomes the only public value. As this planet becomes crowded and even dangerous, our greatest public activity becomes "the exploitation of the solar system." The vaunted freedom of the individual to choose becomes either the necessity of finding one's role in the public engineering or the necessity of retreating into the privacy of pleasure.

Liberalism is the fitting ideology for a society directed toward these ends. It denies unequivocally that there are any given restraints that might hinder pursuit of dynamic dominance. In political terms, liberalism is now an appeal for "the end of ideology." This means that we must experiment in shaping society unhindered by any preconceived notions of good. "The end of ideology" is the perfect slogan for men who want to do what they want. Liberalism is, then, the faith that can understand progress as an extension into the unlimited possibility of the future. It does this much better than Marxism, which still blocks progress by its old-fashioned ideas of the perfectibility of man.

Marxists fail to understand the modern age when they assume that socialism is a more progressive form of organization than state capitalism. Implied in the progressive idea of freedom is the belief that men should emancipate their passions. When men are free to do what they want, all will be well because the liberated desires will be socially creative. This belief lies at the very centre of liberal movements.[16] Marx claimed to be the inheritor of the noblest aspects of liberal thought. He believed that when scientists had eliminated scarcity as the cause of greed and oppression, a society would arise in which the freedom of each to pursue his desires would not conflict with a happy social order. The dictatorship of the proletariat was a passing necessity that would lead into a society of freedom. Under Communism, the passions would be emancipated, but they would be socially useful, not the corrupt passion of greed caused by scarcity. Even those socialists who did not follow Marx in the doctrine of the withering away of the state still generally believed that socialism would create a society of freedom in the sense of the emancipated passions. Socialism was considered an essentially progressive doctrine. It led to freedom.

There is confusion in the minds of those who believe in socialism and the emancipation of the passions. It is surely difficult to deny that greed in some form is a desire that belongs to man *qua* man, and is not simply produced by the society of scarcity. If this is so, to emancipate the passions is to emancipate greed. Yet what is socialism, if it is not the use of the government to restrain greed in the name of social good? In actual practice, socialism has always had to advocate inhibition in this respect.

In doing so, was it not appealing to the conservative idea of social order against the liberal idea of freedom? Even if socialists maintain that their policies would lead in the long run to a society of unrestricted freedom, in the short run they have always been advocates of greater control over freedom. This

16 This last doctrine reminds one of the vast gulf that separates modern moral philosophy from the central teachings of the antique world.

confusion in their thought is the chief reason why socialism has not succeeded in the large technological societies since 1945.

Western civilization was committed in its heart to the religion of progress and the emancipated passions. Those who accepted such a doctrine found corporation capitalism was a much more suitable régime than the inhibiting policies of socialism.[17] Since 1945, Marxist socialism has had its triumphs, but these have been in authoritarian régimes, in societies that needed the discipline of authority in order to industrialize quickly. The triumphs have not been in the West. Early capitalism was full of moral restraints. The Protestant ethic inhibited any passion that did not encourage acquisition. The greed of each would lead to the greatest good for all. But in the age of high technology, the new capitalism can allow all passions to flourish along with greed. *Playboy* illustrates the fact that the young executive is not expected to be Horatio Alger. The titillation of the jaded tastes of the masses serves the purpose of the corporation élites, so long as a sufficient quota of the young is siphoned off as scientists and executives. With automation, the work-ethic of Protestantism disappears. Liberal ideology reconciles the political power of the élites with the private satisfactions of the masses. State capitalism and liberalism are much more advanced manifestations of the age of progress than the Russian system with its official Marxism.

American conservatives also claim that the United States is not the most progressive society on earth. Conservatives maintain that American society retains certain traditional values that have been lost in Communist societies. This claim appeals to history by asserting that the American Revolution was

17 This failure of socialism to recognize itself as an essentially conservative force has nowhere been so patently obvious as in the confusions of the Canadian socialist movement.

essentially conservative – as distinct from the radical revolution in France. The American Revolution did not appeal to the
perfectibility of man but to the traditional rights of Englishmen. At its heart there were the ideals of a constitutional government and the inalienable rights of persons and their
property. It is admitted in such arguments that many who supported the revolution were influenced by French revolutionary
ideas; but at the centre of the Republic were such men as
Washington, Madison, Hamilton, and Adams, rather than
such men as Jefferson and Paine. Edmund Burke castigated the
revolution in France while he defended the American cause.
This indicates the conservatism of the American Revolution.
The claim of conservatives is that bourgeois constitutionalism
has remained the dominant tradition of the Republic despite
the continuing liberal attack.

This argument has at its heart an interpretation of the history of political philosophy with which the present writer
would agree. To put that interpretation simply, modern political philosophy may be divided into two main waves.[18] The
first wave started with Machiavelli and Hobbes and found its
bourgeois expression in such British thinkers as Locke, Smith,
and Hume. The chief originator of the second wave was
Rousseau, and this wave has spread out into the world
through Kant and Hegel. The earlier thinkers criticized the
classical view of nature and natural law, but they still maintained some conception of what was natural. While believing
that man's essence was his freedom, the later thinkers advocated the progressive mastery through that freedom of human
and non-human nature. Man in his freedom was thought to
stand outside nature, and therefore to be able to perfect it. We
could interfere with nature and make it what we wanted. It is

18 For this account of political philosophy see Leo Strauss, *Natural
Right and History* (Chicago: University of Chicago Press, 1953).

from this doctrine that the continuous revolution of the modern era has proceeded.

In applying this interpretation, the American conservatives claim that the United States was founded on the thought of the first wave, while the Communist empires took their ideology from Rousseau and Marx. Therefore the United States should be called a conservative force. The founders of the American Republic were followers of Locke.[19] The assumptions of Locke and Smith are said to have given English-speaking societies stability of constitutional government and freedom from continuous revolution. They escaped the worst results of totalitarianism (call it, if you will, totalitarian democracy) which swept eastward from the continent of Europe. The capitalism of the English-speaking world was stabilized by being founded on a conception of human nature. The doctrine of human nature of Locke and Smith may be inadequate compared to the classical teachings, but it is less destructive of humanity than the later doctrines, which assert that men are completely mal-

---

19 A recent Roman Catholic form of the argument from Locke makes an even fuller claim. It identifies the Lockian thoughts of the nation's founders with the political philosophy of Aquinas. Father Courtney Murray has made the same attempt for the United States that Acton made a century ago in England – the identification of the modern belief in political freedom with Catholic Christianity. Suffice it to say that Locke largely accepted Hobbes's account of the state of nature, while Aquinas accepted the Aristotelian account. How then can their doctrines of natural right be closely identified? Those who make such attempts should surely be asked to read Coleridge's writings on Locke. To find any close identification between Aquinas's and Locke's doctrines of the virtues surely requires a looser reading of both than nationalist prejudice and flattery of the spirit of the age should allow. This branch of Roman Catholic American political philosophy is hardly then to be treated seriously.

leable to perpetual conditioning. Because of the conservative nature of the United States, as against the revolutionary character of the Communist empires, Christianity and Judaism have been able to survive in North America, while they are persecuted in the modern empires of the East. Whatever the imperfections of American government, it remains at least formally constitutional, while the Marxist societies are tyrannies. The United States must be accepted as the guardian of Western values against the perversions of Western revolutionary thought as they have spread into the East.

It is important to point out one effect of this argument on Canada and the United Kingdom. This appeal to Lockian liberalism has been the philosophy of those who have believed that English-speaking unity was the hope of the modern world. The basic assumption of Churchill's life was that the British future lay in its alliance with the United States – the unity of the democratic-capitalist nations.[20] In Canada, this appeal to English-speaking unity has also been used as an argument for the destruction of Canadian independence. In the events around which this writing turns, many conservative Canadians were convinced that Diefenbaker was being false to English-speaking unity in refusing nuclear arms. The Liberal victory was welcomed in the press of the United Kingdom, and Pearson has always appealed to those in England whose hopes lay in the special relation with the United States. Yet it must be pointed out that the argument from English-speaking unity must play an ambiguous role in relation to Canadian nationalism. If Lockian liberalism is the conservatism of the English-speaking peoples, what was there in British conservatism that was not present in the bourgeois thought of Hamilton and

20 Many contemporary English Conservative leaders – Churchill, Macmillan, Hogg, and others – have been born of wealthy American mothers.

Madison? If there was nothing, then the acts of the Loyalists are deprived of all moral significance. Many of the American Tories were Anglicans and knew well that in opposing the revolution they were opposing Locke. They appealed to the older political philosophy of Richard Hooker. They were not, as the liberal Canadian historians have often described them, a mixture of selfish and unfortunate men who chose the wrong side. If there was nothing valuable in the founders of English-speaking Canada, what makes it valuable for Canadians to continue as a nation today?

To return to the general argument. There is some truth in the claim of American conservatives. Their society does preserve constitutional government and respect for the legal rights of individuals in a way that the eastern tyrannies do not. The perpetuation of these depends on the continuing tradition of Lockian liberalism among influential classes. Bourgeois Protestantism, with its Catholic and Jewish imitations, have survived in the United States and give some sense of the eternal to many people. Nevertheless, these traditions – no longer the heart of American civilization – become more residual every year. Sceptical liberalism becomes increasingly the dominant ideology of those who shape society; and, as it was argued earlier, this ideology is the extreme form of progressive modernity. The United States is no longer a society of small property owners, but of massive private and public corporations. Such organizations work with the scientists in their efforts to master nature and reshape humanity. Internationally, the imperial power of these corporations has destroyed indigenous cultures in every corner of the globe. Communist imperialism is more brutally immediate, but American capitalism has shown itself more subtly able to dissolve indigenous societies. This can make it harder to resist than the blatant thrusts of the Russians or the Chinese. The new methods the social sciences use to dissolve the opposition in friendly or enemy societies are welcomed by the government of the United States.[21]

The history of how modern liberalism has replaced the older republican traditions cannot be given in detail. It is not surprising that this should have happened. It was in the West the idea arose that human nature is completely malleable, and this the United States today inherits. American society has also inherited the older aspects of the Western tradition: the Church, constitutional government, classical and philosophical studies. But every day these become more like museum pieces, mere survivals on the periphery.

The Americans who call themselves "Conservatives" have the right to the title only in a particular sense. In fact, they are old-fashioned liberals. They stand for the freedom of the individual to use his property as he wishes, and for a limited government which must keep out of the marketplace. Their concentration on freedom from governmental interference has more to do with nineteenth-century liberalism than with traditional conservatism, which asserts the right of the community to restrain freedom in the name of the common good. Senator Goldwater appealed directly to the American Constitution and to Locke, its philosophical architect. The Senator's chief economic adviser, Professor Milton Friedman, appeals to the British liberal economists of the nineteenth century. They are "conservatives" only in terms of the short history of their own country. They claim that the authentic American tradition went off the rails with the mass liberalism of the New Deal and should return to the individualism of the founding fathers. The makers of the Constitution took their philosophy from the first wave of modernity; the spirit of the New Deal belonged

21 See "Toward a Technology of Human Behaviour for Defense Use" by Charles W. Bray, in *The American Psychologist* (August 1962). This is a synopsis of a report to the American Secretary of Defense.

to the later waves of liberalism. In this sense, Goldwater is an American conservative. But what he conserves is the liberal philosophy of Locke. The founders of the United States took their thought from the eighteenth-century Enlightenment. Their rallying cry was "freedom." There was no place in their cry for the organic conservatism that pre-dated the age of progress. Indeed, the United States is the only society on earth that has no traditions from before the age of progress. Their "right-wing" and "left-wing" are just different species of liberalism. "Freedom" was the slogan of both Goldwater and President Johnson.[22]

The clobbering of Goldwater at the polls in November of 1964 shows how little the American people cared about the early liberalism of their founders. Johnson's "Great Society" expressed the new American "freedom" far better than Goldwater's talk of limited government and free enterprise. The majority tradition in the United States backs Roosevelt, Kennedy, Johnson, whose liberalism is the most modern. The older liberalism of the Constitution had its swan song in the election of 1964. The classes that had once opposed Roosevelt were spent forces by 1964. The leaders of the new capitalism

22 In an earlier day, this was one respect in which Canada could be differentiated from the United States. Canadians had memories of a conservative tradition that was more than covert liberalism. At their best, Canadian conservatives never stood on an abstract appeal to free enterprise. They were willing to use the government to protect the common good. They were willing to restrain the individual's freedom in the interests of the community. The recent conservatism of Toronto, as expressed by the *Globe and Mail*, is American, not Canadian, conservatism. They call for the protection of property from government interference. Canadian Goldwaterism shows how much Toronto is now in spirit a part of the United States.

supported Johnson. Goldwater's cry for limited government seemed as antediluvian to the leaders of the corporations as Diefenbaker's nationalism seemed to the same elements in Canada. Johnson was supported not only by such obvious groups as Negroes and labour but also by the new managerial bourgeoisie of the suburbs. The farmers, who were supposed to be the last bastion of individualism, were not slow in voting for the continuance of subsidies. Four of Goldwater's five states were from the South. This was the last-ditch stand of a local culture. But it is doomed to disappear as much as an indigenous French Canada. The Goldwater camp was outraged by the sustained attacks of the television networks and newspaper chains. Were they not aware who had become the American establishment since 1932? Corporation capitalism and liberalism go together by the nature of things. The establishment knew how to defend itself when threatened by the outrageous challenge of outsiders from Arizona. The American election of 1964 is sufficient evidence that the United States is not a conservative society. It is a dynamic empire spearheading the age of progress.

The foregoing is platitudinous. But one consequence of the argument is not always made explicit: the impossibility of conservatism as a viable political ideology in our era. The practical men who call themselves conservatives must commit themselves to a science that leads to the conquest of nature. This science produces such a dynamic society that it is impossible to conserve anything for long. In such an environment, all institutions and standards are constantly changing. Conservatives who attempt to be practical face a dilemma. If they are not committed to a dynamic technology, they cannot hope to make any popular appeal. If they are so committed, they cannot hope to be conservatives. For example, the most brilliant conservative of our era has only been able to preserve what he loves (the power and culture of France) by gaining support for nationalism from the most advanced technocrats. De Gaulle has had immediate success, but in the long run he will have helped to build a Europe in which the particularities of France cannot hope to exist. Other examples are legion. These days even the Papacy attempts to liberalize itself.

The impossibility of conservatism in our epoch is seen in the fact that those who adopt that title can be no more than the defenders of whatever structure of power is at any moment necessary to technological change. They provide the external force necessary if the society is to be kept together. They are not conservatives in the sense of being the custodians of something that is not subject to change. They are conservatives, generally, in the sense of advocating a sufficient amount of order so the demands of technology will not carry the society into chaos.[23] Because they are advocates of nothing more than this external order, they have come to be thought of as objects of opprobrium by the generous-hearted.

23 The next wave of American "conservatism" is not likely to base its appeal on such unsuccessful slogans as the Constitution and free enterprise. Its leader will not be a gentleman who truly cares about his country's past. It will concentrate directly on such questions as "order in the streets," which are likely to become crucial in the years ahead. The battle will be between democratic tyrants and the authoritarians of the right. If the past is a teacher to the present, it surely says that democratic Caesarism is likely to be successful. In the fight between Sulla and Marius, it was the descendants of the latter who established the Julian line of emperors.

Chapter Six

THE IMPOSSIBILITY OF CONSERVATISM in our era is the impossibility of Canada. As Canadians we attempted a ridiculous task in trying to build a conservative nation in the age of progress, on a continent we share with the most dynamic nation on earth. The current of modern history was against us.

A society only articulates itself as a nation through some common intention among its people. The constitutional arrangements of 1791, and the wider arrangements of the next century, were only possible because of a widespread determination not to become part of the great Republic. Among both the French and the British, this negative intention sprang from widely divergent traditions. What both peoples had in common was the fact they both recognized, that they could only be preserved outside the United States of America. The French were willing to co-operate with the English because they had no alternative but to go along with the endurable arrangements proposed by the ruling power. Both the French and the British had limited common ground in their sense of social order – belief that society required a high degree of law, and respect for a public conception of virtue. Both would grant the state much wider rights to control the individual than was recognized in the libertarian ideas of the American constitution. If their different conservatisms could have become a conscious bond, this nation might have preserved itself. An indigenous society might have continued to exist on the northern half of this continent. To see why this intention failed in Canada, it is necessary to look more closely at the origins of both the French and the British traditions to see what has happened to them. To start with the British, it would be foolish to over-emphasize the niceties of theory among those who came to the St. John Valley or Upper Canada in the late eighteenth and early nineteenth centuries. It is difficult to put into words the conservatism of the English-speaking peoples in the Atlantic colonies or Upper Canada. The manifold waves of differing settlers must not be simplified into any common pattern. Much of English-speaking conservatism was simply a loyalty based on the flow of trade, and therefore destined to change when that flow changed. To repeat, Diefenbaker spoke with telling historical sense when he mentioned the Annexation Manifesto in his last speech to Parliament before the defeat of his government in 1963. He pointed out the similarity between the views of the Montreal merchants in 1849 and the wealthy of Toronto and Montreal in 1963. In neither case did they care about Canada. No small country can depend for its existence on the loyalty of its capitalists. International interests may require the sacrifice of the lesser loyalty of patriotism. Only in dominant nations is the loyalty of capitalists ensured. In such situations, their interests are tied to the strength and vigour of their empire.

This does not imply that the nationalism in English-speaking Canada was simply a front for interest. Many of its elements were shaped by that strange phenomenon, British conservatism, which led the settlers to try to build on the northern half of this continent an independent society. British conservatism is difficult to describe because it is less a clear view of existence than an appeal to an ill-defined past. The writings of Edmund Burke are evidence of this. Yet many of the British officials, many Loyalists, and later many immigrants felt this conservatism very strongly. It was an inchoate desire to build, in these cold and forbidding regions, a society

with a greater sense of order and restraint than freedom-lov- *un defined*
ing republicanism would allow. It was no better defined than
a kind of suspicion that we in Canada could be less lawless
and have a greater sense of propriety than the United States.
The inherited determination not to be Americans allowed
these British people to come to a *modus vivendi* with the more
defined desires of the French. English-speaking Canadians
have been called a dull, stodgy, and indeed costive lot. In these
dynamic days, such qualities are particularly unattractive to
the chic.[24] Yet our stodginess has made us a society of greater
simplicity, formality, and perhaps even innocence than the
people to the south. Whatever differences there were between
the Anglicans and the Presbyterians, and however differently
their theologians might interpret the doctrine of original sin,
both communities believed that the good life made strict
demands on self-restraint. Nothing was more alien to them
than the "emancipation of the passions" desired in American
liberalism. An ethic of self-restraint naturally looks with suspicion on utopian movements, which proceed from an ethic of
freedom. The early leaders of British North America identified
lack of public and personal restraint with the democratic
Republic. Their conservatism was essentially the social doctrine that public order and tradition, in contrast to freedom
and experiment, were central to the good life. The British
Crown was a symbol of a continuing loyalty to the state – less
equivocal than was expected from republicans. In our early
expansions, this conservative nationalism expressed itself in
the use of public control in the political and economic spheres.
Our opening of the West differed from that of the United

24 In his recent book *The Scotch* (New York and Toronto: Macmillan,
1964), Professor J.K. Galbraith has patronized his ancestors from
western Ontario in this vein. A great human advance has been made
from the Presbyterian farm to the sophistication of Harvard.

States, in that the law of the central government was used more extensively, and less reliance was placed on the free settler. Until recently, Canadians have been much more willing than Americans to use governmental control over economic life to protect the public good against private freedom. To repeat, Ontario Hydro, the CNR, and the CBC were all established by Conservative governments. The early establishment of Ontario Hydro succeeded because of the efforts of an administrator, a politician, and a journalist, all of whom wrapped themselves in the Union Jack in their efforts to keep the development of electric power out of the hands of individual freedom.[25]

English-speaking Canadians had never broken with their origins in Western Europe. Many of them had continuing connections with the British Isles, which in the nineteenth century still had ways of life from before the age of progress. That we never broke with Great Britain is often said to prove that we are not a nation but a colony. But the great politicians who believed in this connection – from Joseph Howe and Robert Baldwin to Sir John A. Macdonald and Sir Robert Borden, and indeed to John G. Diefenbaker himself – make a long list. They did not see it this way, but rather as a relation to the font of constitutional government in the British Crown. Many Canadians saw it as a means of preserving at every level of our life – religious, educational, political, social – certain forms of existence that distinguish us from the United States.

To repeat what has been said earlier about the tragedy of Green and Diefenbaker, the end of the Canadian experiment was involved in the collapse of Western Europe, particularly in the disappearance of the British political tradition. Since 1945, the collapse of British power and moral force has been evident

25 The three men were Sir Adam Beck, Sir Richard Whitney, and "Black Jack" Robinson.

to nearly all the world. Its present position is the end-process of that terrible fate that has overtaken Western civilization in the last century. When the British ruling class rushed headlong into the holocaust of 1914, they showed their total lack of political wisdom. As much as anybody, they had been corrupted by the modern mania. Whatever the courage of Churchill in 1940, it must be remembered that he was one of those in the Liberal Cabinet of 1914 who pushed their nation into the intemperance of the earlier disaster. The best British and Canadian youth had their guts torn out in the charnel house of the First World War. To write of the collapse of Western Europe is not my purpose here, but one small result was to destroy Great Britain as an alternative pull in Canadian life.

The history of conservatism in Great Britain has been one of growing emptiness and ambiguity. A political philosophy that is centred on virtue must be a shadowy voice in a technological civilization. When men are committed to technology, they are also committed to continual change in institutions and customs. Freedom must be the first political principle – the freedom to change any order that stands in the way of technological advance. Such a society cannot take seriously the conception of an eternal order by which human actions are measured and defined. For some individuals it remains a heavenly insurance policy. Without the conception of such an order, conservatism becomes nothing but the defence of property rights and chauvinism, attractively packaged as appeal to the past. Great Britain was the chief centre from which the progressive civilization spread around the world. Politically it became the leading imperial power of the West. As Plato saw with unflinching clarity, an imperialistic power cannot have a conservative society as its home base. From Hooker to Coleridge, the English conservatives had less and less influence in their own society. The thinkers who increasingly influenced their society were the liberals, with their clear advocacy of freedom and the knowledge that history was on their side. Practical conservatives continued to exert influence. But the classes and institutions to which they belonged have disappeared. The more honest have simply fought rearguard actions; the more ambitious have twisted conservatism into a façade for class and imperial interests. By the second half of the nineteenth century, appeals to such institutions as the monarchy and the church become little more than the praising of formal rituals, residual customs, and museums. Politicians from Disraeli to Macmillan have applied the term "conservative" to themselves; this was hardly more than a nationalist desire to take as much from the age of progress as they could. Indeed, they were less and less competent to do even this. Canada exported to Great Britain a series of extreme buccaneers who assumed the name "British conservative" during its degenerate era.

British conservatism was already largely a spent force at the beginning of the nineteenth century when English-speaking Canadians were making a nation. By the twentieth century, its adherents in Britain were helping to make their country an island outpost in the American conquest of Europe. Was British conservatism likely, then, to continue as a force to make English-speaking Canada independent? If not, what would? The Laurentian Shield and the Eskimos? British tradition has provided us with certain political and legal institutions, some of which are better than their American counterparts. Our parliamentary and judicial institutions may be preferable to the American system, but there is no deep division of principle. Certainly none of the differences between the two sets of institutions are sufficiently important to provide the basis for an alternative culture on the northern half of this continent.

For all the fruitfulness of the British tradition in nineteenth-century Canada, it did not provide any radically different approach to the questions of industrial civilization. Canadians in particular felt the blessings of technology in an environment so hard that to master it needed courage. But conservatism must languish as technology increases. It was not conceivable that industrial society would be organized along essentially different principles from those to the south. Try to imagine whether Toronto could be a quite dissimilar community from Buffalo or Chicago, or Vancouver from Seattle, and this is to answer the question. What other kind of industrial civilization is likely to appear anywhere on earth, let alone on the northern frontier of Manifest Destiny?

Because of the British tradition, socialist movements have been stronger in Canada than in the United States. But socialism has been a weakening force in Canadian life since 1945. To repeat a previous generalization: democratic socialism is not, as it believed itself to be, the high crest of the wave of the future, but rather a phenomenon from the nineteenth century. Since 1945, the forces that will shape our future in the West show themselves to be bureaucratic state capitalism. The only time when democratic socialism was strong in Canadian industrial society was in Ontario during the utopian days at the end of the Second World War. But the Frost and Robarts régimes have shown what a feeble and transitory phenomenon that was. In Ontario, some form of planned economy was the only conceivable alternative to Americanization. But to have anticipated a socialist Ontario was to hope rather than to predict. Certainly its leadership could not have come from the good-natured utopians who led our socialist parties. They had no understanding of the dependence of socialism and nationalism in the Canadian setting. Their confused optimism is seen in the fact that they have generally acted as if they were "left-wing" allies of the Liberal party. Socialist leadership in Canada has been largely a pleasant remnant of the British nineteenth century – the Protestant tabernacle turned liberal. Such a doctrine was too flaccid to provide any basis for independence.[26]

To turn to the more formidable tradition, the French Canadians are determined to remain a nation. During the nineteenth century, they accepted almost unanimously the leadership of their particular Catholicism – a religion with an ancient doctrine of virtue. After 1789, they maintained their connection with the roots of their civilization through their church and its city, which more than any other in the West held high a vision of the eternal. To Catholics who remain Catholics, whatever their level of sophistication, virtue must be prior to freedom. They will therefore build a society in which the right of the common good restrains the freedom of the individual. Quebec was not a society that would come to terms with the political philosophy of Jefferson or the New England capitalists.

Nevertheless, indigenous cultures are dying everywhere in the modern world. French-Canadian nationalism is a last-ditch stand. The French on this continent will at least disappear from history with more than the smirks and whimpers of their English-speaking compatriots with their flags flying and, indeed, with some guns blazing. The reality of their culture, and their desire not to be swamped, cannot save them from the inexorable facts in the continental case. Solutions vary to

26 A temporary advantage for the New Democratic Party is the fact that the powerful have used their heavy artillery on Diefenbaker. In the meantime they neglected the socialists. In the past, the establishment has been able to keep its hands on both the big parties, which could be substituted for each other when the voters wanted a change. When they have re-established their control in the Conservative party and removed Diefenbaker, this advantage will cease. The farmers are weakening as a force in Canadian life and will not have to be reckoned with in the same way in the future.

the problem of how an autonomous culture can be maintained in Quebec. But all the answers face the same dilemma: Those who want to maintain separateness also want the advantages of the age of progress. These two ends are not compatible, for the pursuit of one negates the pursuit of the other. Nationalism can only be asserted successfully by an identification with technological advance; but technological advance entails the disappearance of those indigenous differences that give substance to nationalism. The solutions to this dilemma, which were attempted in the last few years, illustrate its nature.

One solution was the régime directed by Duplessis. No province in Canada gave more welcoming terms to American capital than the government of Duplessis. At the same time, in questions of education, provincial autonomy, etc., Duplessis followed policies that won support from the rural episcopate. It is all very well for a practising politician to base his régime on the combined support of St. James St. and the traditional Church. The people would depend on the corporations for their employment, while accepting the paternal hand of the cleric in the parish and in the school. Did the clerics think this was the best way for their people to learn to live with industrialism? Surely they recognized that such a régime could not last; it would produce new classes in society ultimately more hostile to Catholicism than to capitalism.

René Lévesque's solution to the problem, unlike Duplessis's liaison with American capitalism, seems to attempt to build a semi-socialist society within the bounds of the province. The idea is to guarantee that the managerial élite be men of French culture, and that the control of the economy rest firmly in native hands. In such a scheme the continuance of Confederation is simply a question of convenience. If French civilization can be protected as a province within Confederation, then all well and good. If it cannot be, then separatism becomes a necessity. Lévesque's brilliant description of Laurier as "a black king" shows the seriousness of his intention.

There are two main difficulties in a semi-socialistic solution. The first of these is symbolized by the presence of Eric Kierans and George Marler as Ministers in the same government as Lévesque. The two men well represent the new and the old establishments of English-speaking Montreal. Provincial control of economic development is not only useful for French-Canadian nationalism but also for international capitalism. Any federal system of government strengthens the power of the corporations. The division of powers weakens the ability of public authority to control private governments; the size of the provinces allows them to be controlled by private economic power. The espousing by American or Canadian "conservatives" of greater authority for the local states has always a phoney ring about it, unless it is coupled with an appeal for the break-up of continental corporations. Decentralized government and continental corporations can lead in only one direction. In his criticism of Walter Gordon's budget in 1963, Kierans made a violent attack against any curbing of foreign investment as being a deterrent to economic growth.[27] As a Minister of the Quebec government, he accepts the thesis that economic growth is chiefly a responsibility of provincial governments. As regards provincial responsibility, Lévesque and Kierans are in agreement, but their motives for espousing responsibility are quite different. The motive of quick industrializing is surely likely to come in conflict with the motive of nationalism.

The financial pages of every newspaper are filled with announcements of French-speaking appointments to management. Continental capitalists have learnt that they are going to

27 Kierans repeated this attack in a speech in Toronto in December of 1963.

be in trouble if such appointments are not made. But when French nationalists derive satisfaction from these appointments, they would do well to remind themselves of the ancient adage: "I fear the Greeks, especially when they come with gifts." Corporations make concessions about management personnel for the sake of better relations with the alien community. These do not involve the basic control of the economy. Here the lines of battle will surely be drawn. How long will the people of Quebec be willing to pay the economic price of rejecting the terms laid down by big business for the development of power at Hamilton Falls? It is not likely that even such an unusual Liberal government as that of Prime Minister Lesage will be able to wrest control of the economy from the corporations and then keep it in the government's hands.[28]

The concession over French managerial personnel points to a greater chink in the nationalist armour. Lévesque presumably believes that the indigenous control of the French-Canadian economy will be maintained by the vote. Governments will retain final control of their economies through Socialistic measures by seeking electoral support. But is it to be expected that the new managerial élites will sustain their French culture for very long? If they work for continental corporations, will they not identify themselves with those corporations and vote for governments not interested in preserving national control of the economy? This is what happened in Ontario in the 1940s and 1950s. Even when much of the economy is socialized, the man-

28 The difference between the federal and provincial parties is wide, but not that wide. Indeed, Lévesque won a great victory when the provincial Liberals voted in their convention of 1964 that their party did not owe allegiance to the federal organization. Lévesque spent the federal election of 1963 in France. Presumably he could not stomach the policy of the federal Liberals on nuclear arms. His absence was a sop he had to pay for his membership in the party.

agers will gradually become indistinguishable from their international counterparts. To run a modern economy, men must be
trained in the new technology over human and non-human
nature. Such training cannot be reconciled with French-Canadian classical education. An élite trained in the modern way may
speak French for many generations, but what other traditions
will it uphold? The new social sciences are dissolvents of the
family, of Catholicism, of classical education. It is surely more
than a language that Lévesque wishes to preserve in his nation.
New Orleans is a pleasant place for tourists. The dilemma
remains. French Canadians must modernize their educational
system if they are to have more than a peon's place in their own
industrialization. Yet to modernize their education is to renounce
their particularity. At the heart of modern liberal education lies
the desire to homogenize the world. Today's natural and social
sciences were consciously produced as instruments to this end.

In the immediate future, the wilder of the nationalist
French-Canadian youths may hope to build some kind of Cas-
tro-like state in Quebec. As traditional Catholicism breaks up,
there will be some exciting moments. A Catholic society cannot be modernized as easily as a Protestant one. When the dam
breaks the flood will be furious. Nevertheless, the young intellectuals of the upper-middle class will gradually desert their
existentialist nationalism and take the places made for them in
the continental corporations. The enormity of the break from
the past will arouse in the dispossessed youth intense forms of
beatness. But after all, the United States supports a large beat
fringe. Joan Baez and Pete Seeger titillate the *status quo* rather
than threaten it. Dissent is built into the fabric of the modern
system. We bureaucratize it as much as everything else. Is there
any reason to believe that French Canada will be different? A
majority of the young is gradually patterned for its place in the
bureaucracies. Those who resist such shaping will retreat into
a fringe world of pseudo-revolt.

What does Lévesque think is the place of Catholicism in the

continuing French fact? The young French Canadians who desire a better society, because they grew up under Duplessis, believe in both nationalism and social freedom. Their liberalism is openly anti-Catholic and even existentialist or Marxist. Others accept Catholicism but are determined that the Church should be disestablished. But the old Church with its educational privileges has been the chief instrument by which an indigenous French culture has survived in North America. Liberalism is the ideological means whereby indigenous cultures are homogenized. How then can nationalism and liberalism merge together into a consistent political creed?

In 1918, Bourassa put the purposes of French-Canadian existence in clear words:

> *Notre tâche à nous, Canadiens-français, c'est de prolonger en Amérique l'effort de la France chrétienne; c'est de défendre contre tout venant, le fallût-il contre la France elle-même, notre patrimoine religieux et national. Ce patrimoine, il n'est pas à nous seulement: il appartient à toute l'Amérique catholique, dont il est le foyer inspirateur et rayonnant; il appartient à toute l'Église, dont il est le principal point d'appui dans cette partie du monde; il appartient à toute la civilisation française, dont il est l'unique port de refuge et d'attache dans cette mer immense de l'américanisme saxonisant.*[29]

29 See H. Bourassa, *La Langue, gardienne de la Foi* (Montreal, 1918). Freely translated: "Our special task as French Canadians, is to insert into America the spirit of Christian France. It is to defend against all comers, perhaps even against France herself, our religious and national heritage. This heritage does not belong to us alone. It belongs to all Catholic America. It is the inspiring and shining hearth of that America. It belongs to the whole Church, and it is the basic foundation of the Church in this part of the world. It belongs to all French civilization of which it is the refuge and anchor amid the immense sea of saxonizing Americanism."

Here is a national intention, beautifully expressed.

Bourassa's clarity about this intention was not matched by his understanding of what the twentieth century was going to be. He considered North America to be essentially *saxonisant* and dominated by an explicitly Protestant ethos – the "time is money" theology of a debased and secularized Calvinism. He lived in a world in which the British Empire still appeared a dominant force. Presumably he still thought of Latin America as in that twilight period of subservience to North America, which extended from the beginning of the nineteenth century.[30] Above all, Bourassa does not seem to have been aware of the effect of homogenization – what industrial civilization would do to all countries and all religions. Industrial culture had arisen in Protestant societies and was the very form of *américanisme saxonisant* that surrounded his nation. Bourassa seems therefore to have identified the two, rather than to have recognized that technological culture was a dissolvent of all national and religious traditions, not simply an expression of one of them. There is little of Gandhi's rejection of industrialism in his writings, but rather the positive assumption that the culture of Quebec was French Christianity.[31] Nationalism was for him something essentially conservative – the maintenance in his part of the world of the true way of life against the heresy of *américanisme saxonisant*. This was a wasting and tragic dream for our dynamic era. Nevertheless, despite his unawareness of the dynamism of the twentieth century, he was surely right when he said that

30 In Latin America there were 62 million in 1900, 120 million in 1950, 205 million in 1960. In the year 1955, North America ceased to have more people than South America.

31 France herself has always been a middle term between the dynamic civilization of Northern Europe and the more static culture of the Mediterranean.

Catholicism as well as Frenchness was necessary to make Quebec a nation.

Dynamic civilization has spread like oil over the surface of the world during the half-century since Bourassa wrote. The twentieth century is not something that belongs essentially to *l'américanisme saxonisant*. It is no longer potential but actual in Quebec. Indeed, a wider question arises here: What is the status of Catholicism in the age of progress? Will a liberalized Catholicism accept industrialism and still be able to shape it to a more human end? In Quebec, Catholicism will no longer be "*Je me souviens*," but a Catholicism appropriate to a vital present. Lay education will not destroy the Church, but enable her to become the spiritual leader of a free people. Accepting the age of progress, the Church will give leadership to a more humane industrialism than has arisen elsewhere in North America. It will provide the spiritual basis for a continuing Franco-American civilization.

The possibility of such a Catholicism in Quebec cannot be discussed apart from the relation of Catholicism to technology throughout the world. That intricate question cannot be discussed at length in this writing. Suffice it to say that, although the recent statements of the Papacy seem optimistic about the Church's ability to live with our age, it is still an open question whether Catholicism will be able to humanize mass Western society or be swept into the catacombs. What happens to the Catholic view of man, when Catholics are asked to shape society through the new sciences of biochemistry, physiological psychology, and sociology? These sciences arose from assumptions hostile to the Catholic view of man. Whatever the historical outcome, the ability of Catholicism to sustain a continuing Franco-American civilization appears dubious. If liberal Catholicism arises in Quebec, will it not be similar to the Catholicism of Cushing and Spellman, which is well-established within the assumptions of the American

Empire?[32] Such a religion may have the same name, but it will be very different from the one Bourassa envisaged. The Church in America does not question the assumption of the society that permits it, except in the most general way. With this kind of Catholicism, industrialized Quebec would hardly be distinguishable from the rest of North America. Yet this is what the leading liberal clerics and laity seem to be establishing in the province. With such a moral heart, Quebec will soon blend into the continental whole and cease to be a nation except in its maintenance of residual patterns of language and personal habit.

Levesque, at least, appears to be aware how difficult it will be to preserve the French fact on this continent. The French-Canadian liberals who plead for the continuance of Confederation and the extension of co-operative federalism seem to be more naive. The confusion of these French-Canadian liberals is evident in a recent pronouncement by seven French-Canadian intellectuals under the title "An Appeal for Realism in Politics."[33] This pronouncement is considered by its authors to be a Canadian – not a French-Canadian – manifesto. It is an appeal for the continuance of Confederation against the various parochialisms that threaten it. It puts forward the hope for a vital federalism that will accept the cultural diversity of Canada but will not be economically nationalist. It is not my purpose here to discuss its detailed proposals, but to quote its philosophical justification as an example of the present

32 It is hard to imagine what Bourassa would have thought of the fact that it was a Catholic President of the United States of America (albeit a Teddy Roosevelt Catholic) who successfully applied pressure on the Canadian people for the acquisition of nuclear arms.

33 This manifesto was published concurrently in French in *Cité Libre*, Montreal, and in English in *The Canadian Forum* (May, 1964), Toronto.

thought of French-Canadian liberal intellectuals. At the end of the manifesto, two reasons are given why the writers refuse to be "locked into a constitutional frame smaller than Canada." The second reason for this is described in the following language:

> *The most valid trends today are toward more enlightened humanism, toward various forms of political, social, and economic universalism. Canada is a reproduction on a smaller and simpler scale of this universal phenomenon. The challenge is for a number of ethnic groups to learn to live together. It is a modern challenge, meaningful and indicative of what can be expected from man. If Canadians cannot make a success of a country such as theirs, how can they contribute in any way to the elaboration of humanism, to the formulation of the international structures of tomorrow? To confess one's inability to make Canadian Confederation work is, at this stage of history, to admit one's unworthiness to contribute to the universal order.*

Leaving aside such questions as what makes a trend "valid" and what are the conditions of human enlightenment, the point at issue is that the authors assert their faith in universalism and in the continued existence of Canada at one and the same time. The faith in universalism makes it accurate to call the authors liberal. But how can a faith in universalism go with a desire for the continuance of Canada? The belief in Canada's continued existence has always appealed against universalism. It appealed to particularity against the wider loyalty to the continent. If universalism is the most "valid modern trend," then is it not right for Canadians to welcome our integration into the empire? Canadian nationalism is a more universal faith than French-Canadian nationalism. But if one is a universalist, why should one stop at that point of particularity?

Many French-Canadian liberals seem to espouse "enlightened humanism" and universalism as against the parochial Catholicism that inhibited them personally and politically when it ruled their society. They seem to expect liberalism to purge Catholicism, but to maintain within itself all that was best in the ancient faith. In this manifesto, for example, the authors espouse the continuance of indigenous cultures and regret the victimizing of the "Indians, Metis, Orientals, Doukhobors, Hutterites, and dissidents of all kinds" in our past. They call for the democratic protection of such cultures. But do they not know that liberalism in its most unequivocal form (that is, untinged by memories of past traditions) includes not only the idea of universalism but also that of homogeneity? The high rhetoric of democracy was used when the Doukhobors were "victimized" under a French-Canadian Prime Minister. If the writers are to be truly liberal, they cannot escape the fact that the goal of their political philosophy is the universal and homogeneous state. If this is the noblest goal, then the idea of Canada was a temporary and misguided parochialism. Only those who reject that goal and claim that the universal state will be a tyranny, that is, a society destructive of human excellence, can assert consistently that parochial nationalisms are to be fought for. My purpose is not to debate at this point the question whether the "universal" values of liberalism lead to human excellence. What is indubitable is that those values go with internationalism rather than with nationalism. In this century, many men have known that the choice between internationalism and nationalism is the same choice as that between liberalism and conservatism. In a Canadian setting, internationalism means continentalism. French-Canadian liberalism does not seem to be the means whereby this nation could have been preserved.

All the preceding arguments point to the conclusion that Canada cannot survive as a sovereign nation. In the language of the new bureaucrats, our nation was not a viable entity. If one adds to this proposition the memory of the Liberals' policies, then one can truly say that the argument in their favour succeeds. They have been the best rulers for Canada because they have led the majority of us to accept necessity without much pain. *Fata volentem ducunt, nolentem trahunt.* Fate leads the willing, and drives the unwilling. The debt that we owe the Liberals is that they have been so willing to be led. The party has been made up of those who put only one condition on their willingness: that they should have personal charge of the government while our sovereignty disappears.

Canada has ceased to be a nation, but its formal political existence will not end quickly. Our social and economic blending into the empire will continue apace, but political union will probably be delayed. Some international catastrophe or great shift of power might speed up this process. Its slowness does not depend only on the fact that large numbers of Canadians do not want it, but also on sheer lethargy. Changes require decisions, and it is much easier for practising politicians to continue with traditional structures. The dominant forces in the Republic do not need to incorporate us. A branch-plant satellite, which has shown in the past that it will not insist on any difficulties in foreign or defence policy, is a pleasant arrangement for one's northern frontier. The pinpricks of disagreement are a small price to pay. If the negotiations for union include Quebec, there will be strong elements in the United States that will dislike their admission. The kindest of all God's dispensations is that individuals cannot predict the future in detail. Nevertheless, the formal end of Canada may be prefaced by a period during which the government of the United States has to resist the strong desire of English-speaking Canadians to be annexed.

Chapter Seven

PERHAPS WE SHOULD REJOICE in the disappearance of Canada. We leave the narrow provincialism and our backwoods culture; we enter the excitement of the United States where all the great things are being done. Who would compare the science, the art, the politics, the entertainment of our petty world to the overflowing achievements of New York, Washington, Chicago, and San Francisco? Think of William Faulkner and then think of Morley Callaghan. Think of the Kennedys and the Rockefellers and then think of Pearson and E.P. Taylor. This is the profoundest argument for the Liberals. They governed so as to break down our parochialism and lead us into the future.

Before discussing this position, I must dissociate myself from a common philosophic assumption. I do not identify necessity and goodness. This identification is widely assumed during an age of progress. Those who worship "evolution" or "history" consider that what must come in the future will be "higher," "more developed," "better," "freer" than what has been in the past. This identification is also common among those who worship God according to Moses or the Gospels. They identify necessity and good within the rubric of providence. From the assumption that God's purposes are unfolded in historical events, one may be led to view history as an ever-fuller manifestation of good. Since the tenth century of the Christian era, some Western theologians have tended to interpret the fallen sparrow as if particular events could be apprehended by faith as good. This doctrine of providence was given its best philosophical expression by Hegel: "*Die Welt-geschichte ist das Weltgericht*" – "World history is the world's judgement." Here the doctrines of progress and providence have been brought together. But if history is the final court of appeal, force is the final argument. Is it possible to look at history and deny that within its dimensions force is the supreme ruler? To take a progressive view of providence is to come close to worshipping force. Does this not make us cavalier about evil? The screams of the tortured child can be justified by the achievements of history. How pleasant for the achievers, but how meaningless for the child.

As a believer, I must then reject these Western interpretations of providence. Belief is blasphemy if it rests on any easy identification of necessity and good. It is plain that there must be other interpretations of the doctrine. However massive the disaster we might face – for example, the disappearance of constitutional government for several centuries, or the disappearance of our species – belief in providence should be unaffected. It must be possible within the doctrine of providence to distinguish between the necessity of certain happenings and their goodness. A discussion of the goodness of Canada's disappearance must therefore be separated from a discussion of its necessity.

Many levels of argument have been used to say that it is good that Canada should disappear. In its simplest form, continentalism is the view of those who do not see what all the fuss is about. The purpose of life is consumption, and therefore the border is an anachronism. The forty-ninth parallel results in a lower standard of living for the majority to the north of it. Such continentalism has been an important force throughout Canadian history. Until recently it was limited by two factors. Emigration to the United States was not too difficult for Canadians, so that millions were able to seek their fuller future to the south. Moreover, those who believed in the primacy of private prosperity have generally been too concerned with individual pursuits to bother with political advocacy. Nevertheless, this spirit is bound to grow. One has only to live in the Niagara peninsula to understand it. In the mass era, most human beings are defined in terms of their capacity to consume. All other differences between them, like political traditions, begin to appear unreal and unprogressive. As consumption becomes primary, the border appears an anachronism, and a frustrating one at that.

The disadvantages in being a branch-plant satellite rather than in having full membership in the Republic will become obvious. As the facts of our society substantiate continentalism, more people will explicitly espouse it. A way of life shaped by continental institutions will produce political continentalism. Young and ambitious politicians will arise to give tongue to it. The election of 1963 was the first time in our history that a strongly nationalist campaign did not succeed, and that a government was brought down for standing up to the Americans. The ambitious young will not be slow to learn the lesson that Pearson so ably taught them about what pays politically. Some of the extreme actions of French Canadians in their efforts to preserve their society will drive other Canadians to identify themselves more closely with their southern neighbours than with the strange and alien people of Quebec.

Of course continentalism was more than a consumption-ideology. In the nineteenth century, the United States appeared to be the haven of opportunity for those who had found no proper place in the older societies. Men could throw off the shackles of inequality and poverty in the new land of opportunity. To many Canadians, the Republic seemed a freer and more open world than the costive colonial society with its restraints of tradition and privilege. The United States appeared to be the best society the world had ever produced for the ordinary citizen. Whatever the mass society of prosperity has become, the idea that the United States is the society of freedom, equality, and opportunity will continue to stir many hearts. The affection and identification that a vast majority of Canadians have given to the publicly expressed ideals of such leaders as Roosevelt and Kennedy is evidence of this. Continentalism as a philosophy is based on the liberal interpretation of history. Because much of our intellectual life has been oriented to Great Britain, it is not surprising that our chief continentalists have been particularly influenced by British liberalism. The writings of Goldwin Smith and F.H. Underhill carry more the note of Mill and Macaulay than of Jefferson and Jackson. This continentalism has made two main appeals. First, Canadians need the greater democracy of the Republic. To the continentalists, both the French and British traditions in Canada were less democratic than the social assumptions of the United States. In such arguments, democracy has not been interpreted solely in a political sense, but has been identified with social equality, contractual human relations, and the society open to all men, regardless of race or creed or class. American history is seen to be the development of the first mass democracy on earth.[34] The second appeal of continentalism is that humanity requires that nationalisms be overcome. In moving to larger units of government, we are moving in the direction of world order. If Canadians refuse this, they are standing back from the vital job of building a peaceful world. After the horrors that nationalistic wars have inflicted on this century, how can one have any sympathy for nationalism? Thank God the world is moving beyond such divisive loyalties.

34 In our generation this interpretation is expounded at length in the sermons of Arthur Schlesinger, Jr.

Both these arguments were used with particular literacy by F.H. Underhill in his appeals for the Liberal party in the *Toronto Star* at the time of the 1963 election.[35] In his use of both these arguments it was sometimes difficult to know whether Underhill was appealing to the order of good or to the order of necessity, or whether in his mind the two were identical. For example, closeness to the United States was identified in this writing with true internationalism. The argument from necessity is that nationalism must disappear and that we are moving inevitably to a world of continental empires. But this inevitable movement does not in itself mean that we are moving to a better and more peaceful world order. The era of continental rivalries may be more ferocious than the era of nationalisms. Only when one adds to this argument the liberal faith in progress does one believe that continentalism must be a step toward a nobler internationalism. The argument for continentalism is different when it appeals to inevitability than when it is based on the brotherhood of man. This ambiguity in Underhill was mirrored in the whole Liberal campaign of 1963, in which Pearson wrapped his acceptance of continental

35 Professor F.H. Underhill is a key figure in the intellectual history of Canadian liberalism. See his book *In Search of Canadian Liberalism* (Toronto: Macmillan, 1960). Underhill gave many years to building the CCF. He found himself on the opposite side from the business community in Toronto on nearly every public question. Yet in a speech in Toronto in 1964, he could in his seventies announce that the liberal hope lies now with the great corporations. This conversion surely shows how consistently he continues to work out the consequences of his thought. He has recognized that the business community in America is no longer the propertied classes of his youth but managers whose ideology is liberal. He is right to believe that corporations and not doctrinaire socialism are the wave of the future.

atomic arms in the language of international obligations and his loyalty to the United Nations.

To those outside the progressive view of history, there was a note of high comedy in the use of the Tennysonian "parliament of man" language to attack Diefenbaker's defence of national sovereignty, when the issue at stake was the acquisition of nuclear arms. The Sifton and Southam papers made any fear of dominance by the American Empire seem a retreat from true internationalism. This note of comedy went further in the summer of 1963, when the CBC made misty-eyed television programs about Pearson's return to the United Nations as the true Canadian internationalist, at a time when he was negotiating with the United States for the spread of nuclear arms to Canada.

However, laughter should not allow us to fail in charity toward liberalism. It was easier to use its language consistently in the era of Goldwin Smith than in the twentieth century. Liberalism was, in origin, criticism of the old established order. Today it is the voice of the establishment. It could sound a purer note when it was the voice of the outsider than today when it is required to legislate freedom. For example, Harvard liberalism was surely nobler when William James opposed the Spanish-American war than when Arthur Schlesinger, Jr., advised Kennedy on Cuban policy.

It has already been argued that, because of our modern assumptions about human good, Canada's disappearance is necessary.[36] In deciding whether continentalism is good, one is

---

36 In our day, necessity is often identified with some fad in the atoms or the "life force." But historical necessity is chiefly concerned with what the most influential souls have thought about human good. Political philosophy is not some pleasant cultural game reserved for those too impotent for practice. It is concerned with judgements about goodness. As these judgements are apprehended and acted upon by practical men, they become the unfolding of fate.

making a judgement about progressive political philosophy and its interpretation of history. Those who dislike continentalism are in some sense rejecting that progressive interpretation. It can only be with an enormous sense of hesitation that one dares to question modern political philosophy. If its assumptions are false, the age of progress has been a tragic aberration in the history of the species. To assert such a proposition lightly would be the height of irresponsibility. Has it not been in the age of progress that disease and overwork, hunger and poverty, have been drastically reduced? Those who criticize our age must at the same time contemplate pain, infant mortality, crop failures in isolated areas, and the sixteen-hour day. As soon as that is said, facts about our age must also be remembered: the increasing outbreaks of impersonal ferocity, the banality of existence in technological societies, the pursuit of expansion as an end in itself. Will it be good for men to control their genes? The possibility of nuclear destruction and mass starvation may be no more terrible than that of man tampering with the roots of his humanity. Interference with human nature seems to the moderns the hope of a higher species in the ascent of life; to others it may seem that man in his pride could corrupt his very being. The powers of manipulation now available may portend the most complete tyranny imaginable. At least, it is feasible to wonder whether modern assumptions may be basically inhuman.

To many modern men, the assumptions of this age appear inevitable, as being the expression of the highest wisdom that the race has distilled. The assumptions appear so inevitable that to entertain the possibility of their falsity may seem the work of a madman. Yet these assumptions were made by particular men in particular settings. Machiavelli and Hobbes, Spinoza and Vico, Rousseau and Hegel, Marx and Darwin, originated this account of human nature and destiny. Their view of social excellence was reached in conscious opposition to that of the ancient philosophers. The modern account of human nature and destiny was developed from a profound criticism of what Plato and Aristotle had written. The modern thinkers believed that they had overcome the inadequacies of ancient thought, while maintaining what was true in the ancients.

Yet Plato and Aristotle would not have admitted that their teachings could be used in this way. They believed that their own teaching was the complete teaching for all men everywhere, or else they were not philosophers. They believed that they had considered all the possibilities open to man and had reached the true doctrine concerning human excellence. Only the thinkers of the age of progress considered the classical writers as a preparation for the perfected thought of their own age. The classical philosophers did not so consider themselves. To see the classics as a preparation for later thought is then to think within the assumptions of the age of progress. But this is to beg the question, when the issue at stake is whether these assumptions are true. It is this very issue that is raised by the tragedies and ambiguities of our day.[37] Ancient philosophy gives alternative answers to modern man concerning the questions of human nature and destiny. It touches all the central questions that man has asked about himself and the world. The classical philosophers asserted that a universal and homogeneous state would be a tyranny. To elucidate their

37   The previous paragraph is dependent on the writings of Professor Leo Strauss who teaches at the University of Chicago. For Strauss's account of political philosophy, see, for example, *What Is Political Philosophy* (Glencoe: The Free Press, 1959) and *The City and Man* (Chicago: Rand McNally, 1964). I only hope that nothing in the foregoing misinterprets the teaching of that wise man.

argument would require an account of their total teaching concerning human beings. It would take one beyond political philosophy into the metaphysical assertion that changes in the world take place within an eternal order that is not affected by them. This implies a definition of human freedom quite different from the modern view that freedom is man's essence. It implies a science different from that which aims at the conquest of nature.

The discussion of issues such as these is impossible in a short writing about Canada. Also, the discussion would be inconclusive, because I do not know the truth about these ultimate matters. Therefore, the question as to whether it is good that Canada should disappear must be left unsettled. If the best social order is the universal and homogeneous state, then the disappearance of Canada can be understood as a step toward that order. If the universal and homogeneous state would be a tyranny, then the disappearance of even this indigenous culture can be seen as the removal of a minor barrier on the road to that tyranny. As the central issue is left undecided, the propriety of lamenting must also be left unsettled.

My lament is not based on philosophy but on tradition. If one cannot be sure about the answer to the most important questions, then tradition is the best basis for the practical life. Those who loved the older traditions of Canada may be allowed to lament what has been lost, even though they do not know whether or not that loss will lead to some greater political good. But lamentation falls easily into the vice of self-pity. To live with courage is a virtue, whatever one may think of the dominant assumptions of one's age. Multitudes of human beings through the course of history have had to live when their only political allegiance was irretrievably lost. What was lost was often something far nobler than what Canadians have lost. Beyond courage, it is also possible to live in the ancient faith, which asserts that changes in the world, even if they be recognized more as a loss than a gain, take place within an eternal order that is not affected by their taking place. Whatever the difficulty of philosophy, the religious man has been told that process is not all. "*Tendebantque manus ripae ulterioris amore.*"[38]

38 Virgil, *Aeneid* (Book VI): "They were holding their arms outstretched in love toward the further shore."

Afterword

SHEILA GRANT

GEORGE GRANT ALWAYS CLAIMED that *Lament for a Nation* had been misunderstood. At first it was taken by the New Left as a call to nationalism. Since then, the less optimistic political implications have been well documented. This postscript will concentrate on chapter 7, the final chapter. This chapter has been almost entirely ignored. The New Left did not understand it and simply overlooked it. Reviewers during the last thirty years seem to have had the same reaction. Those few who have mentioned it have seen it as further evidence of Grant's "implacable pessimism" and obscurity.

After the extreme clarity of the rest of the book, the tone is indeed different. Grant starts with a statement that he does not share the philosophic assumption that the necessary and the good are inseparably united. This assumption implies that history records the triumph of the good – that progress is inevitable and visible. Grant shows forcefully the moral nonsense involved in this view of history. He associates it with Hegel, who saw history as the unfolding of reason, and with certain Christian theologians who have held that Providence is understandable, taking in the screams of the tortured child as part of the divine harmony. Grant rejects such a view of history, or of Providence, as blasphemous.

The assertion that there is a distance between the necessary and the good is a difficult, subtle idea, and cannot be explained further here. It does not neutralize all difficulties with regard to the evil in the world. Some readers will disagree with it, some will know they do not understand it. Some may choose to follow its development in Grant's later work. But if it is a basic assumption underlying the writing of *Lament for a Nation*, it should at least not be ignored, if the political parts of the book are to be properly understood in their spiritual as well as their topical significance.

Those readers who see Grant as a relentless pessimist may object that his denial of inevitable progress, and his assertion of a distance between the necessary and the good, themselves imply a grim view of the world. However, it is less grim, surely, than a view which covers up and denies the pain and evil which human beings suffer.

The judgment of political events is always ambiguous. That one's country might cease to be independent is clearly a sad prospect for its citizens. But it is hard to judge whether this would be in the end a greater cause of good, or of ill. Our perspectives are limited. The fact that it happened would in no way prove it to be a good thing.

Grant's lack of pessimism is perhaps best shown in one of his simplest statements, repeated throughout his life, "It always matters what each of us does." It matters not only because of the possible results of our actions but because we are all free to turn towards good action, however difficult that choice may be. For one who believes, as Grant did, that the spiritual life is open to all, pessimism is not an option.

The very end of chapter 7 has also been called pessimistic. It has even been suggested that Grant was desiring his own death. An accusation of obscurity is less easily denied. A line from Virgil is indeed an unexpected way to end a book about Canadian politics. Some readers see it as a stroke of genius; others as a self-indulgent obscurity.

The quoted line comes from a passage in book six of the *Aeneid*, which describes a sinister region, dark and formless ("per vacuas domos Ditis et inania regna"), from which the crowd of departed spirits are begging Charon to rescue them. There is no suggestion of despair, but only hope and longing for a better part of the underworld.

Readers might have preferred Grant to have used more rational language to express this universal longing for a better world. He could have done so by means of another of his favourite quotations (attributed to St. Augustine): "Out of the shadows and imaginings into the truth" ("ex umbris et imaginibus in veritatem"). The thought is similar but Virgil's poetic image is more universal. We may not all be desiring the truth but most of us are holding out our arms in longing for some good we desire. In the context of *Lament for a Nation*, we may be longing for a happier life, a stronger country, the survival of our traditions, and leaders we can trust – all various aspects of human good. Grant had a particular way of absorbing a favourite quotation into his own thought, giving it a special weight, without much concern for its original context. In this case, the image of holding out one's arms in longing for a further shore took on a deeply personal significance, as well as the more abstract one. He identified it with the place he loved most, Terence Bay, on the Atlantic coast, all sea and rock. Its austere and unchanging beauty became for him an image of the timeless: a holy place. From a cabin he built on a hill, he would look across the ocean inlet to the towering rocks on the further shore, and quote the line that ends *Lament for a Nation*.

Grant may indeed be blamed for the obscurity of personal association in ending his book as he did. But the accusation of pessimism cannot be substantiated.

Halifax, NS,
January 1997

About the Author

George P. Grant (1918-1988) was educated at Queen's University and Oxford. He taught philosophy and later political science at Dalhousie University and chaired the Department of Religion at McMaster. One of the foremost Canadian political thinkers of our time, he was the author of *Philosophy in the Mass Age* (1959), *Technology and Empire* (1969), *English-Speaking Justice* (1974), and *Technology and Justice* (1986), as well as the seminal *Lament for a Nation* (1965).